Johann Joseph Ignaz von Döllinger, Franz Heinrich Reusch

Declarations and Letters on the Vatican Decrees

Johann Joseph Ignaz von Döllinger, Franz Heinrich Reusch

Declarations and Letters on the Vatican Decrees

ISBN/EAN: 9783743325753

Manufactured in Europe, USA, Canada, Australia, Japa

Cover: Foto ©ninafisch / pixelio.de

Manufactured and distributed by brebook publishing software (www.brebook.com)

Johann Joseph Ignaz von Döllinger, Franz Heinrich Reusch

Declarations and Letters on the Vatican Decrees

DECLARATIONS AND LETTERS

ON THE

VATICAN DECREES

1869-1887

BY

IGNAZ VON DÖLLINGER.

AUTHORISED TRANSLATION.

EDINBURGH:
T. & T. CLARK, 38 GEORGE STREET.
1891.

PREFACE BY THE EDITOR.

---o---

ON the 2nd October 1886 the late Dr. Döllinger wrote to me as follows:—

"But a very short time ago I received from several quarters intimations that I ought to submit myself. These intimations consist of two verbal communications closely succeeding each other from the Pope, a written one from the Archbishop of Munich (worded very politely and delicately), and a second one in writing from Bishop Hefele. I myself feel very keenly that, before my life's hour-glass runs out, I still owe the world a well-substantiated declaration. There is still so much to be said on the matter that has hitherto not been said, or has only been broached in an enfeebled form, that I cannot dismiss the affair in a pamphlet, but rather am compelled to bring forward in a certain degree of completeness an *aciem argumentorum et factorum instructam*.[1] There are also some personal experiences (about my visit to Rome, and what I saw there) to be narrated. As a

[1] A well-ordered array of arguments and facts.

preliminary step I have carefully weighed the whole subject, and the material is collected. .... The form is to be that of a series of letters addressed to a prelate in high office, whose name, however, out of regard for the man, I should not mention. This affords freer scope. As title I propose to myself, *The Vatican Decrees in the Light of History*. Among other things I think of giving a survey of the dogmatic history of the Roman See from its beginning to the present day, in which history all somewhat important *decreta fidei* that have been issued by a pope would be brought forward, and, where necessary, critically though briefly discussed. As is well known, nothing of this kind exists as yet. Since I received the above-mentioned intimations, this plan has been daily, almost hourly, engaging my attention, so that it is difficult for me to direct my thoughts earnestly to anything else. Partly on this account and partly also because of other hindrances, I must beg you to have patience with me a little longer in reference to the article on Ignatius.[1]

"The considerations, the thinking over of the plan, the enormous quantity of facts and doctrines to be brought forward, which have thrust themselves upon my memory, have been so overwhelming during these last few weeks, that it has been almost too

---

[1] For *The Autobiography of Cardinal Bellarmine*, which appeared in the following year, 1887, at Bonn.

much for me. Now that my mind is clear about the plan, I feel myself free, and disposed to work at the article on Ignatius."

Preparations for these " Letters" have been found among the literary remains of the deceased ; but, as it seems, he was distracted by other work, and did not even begin the compiling of them for publication.

In October 1887, Döllinger showed me a letter he had just received from the Nuncio then in office, together with his own reply, and also a longer letter which he had addressed some months previously to the late Archbishop of Munich. On this occasion he made the remark, that as these letters supplemented each other in vindication of his attitude to the Vatican Decrees, he thought, if an opportunity offered itself, that he would have his letters to the Nuncio and the Archbishop printed, as well as the answers he had sent to two other proselytising letters, the one from a lady of high rank and the other from a nun — Bishop Hefele's letter on the same subject he had left unanswered. It is then fully in accordance with the intentions of the deceased if I now give publicity to the three letters to the Nuncio, the Archbishop, and the lady of high rank,—the one to the nun was not found among Döllinger's literary remains, — together with the letters by which they were occasioned.

Contrary to my original intention, I have had

Bishop Hefele's letter printed along with the others, because the sender himself has given his sanction, and because it was intimated in an article copied in several newspapers that Döllinger's friends presumably would not dare to publish this letter which has been left unanswered by him.

It will be considered opportune that with these hitherto unpublished letters, those declarations and letters on the same subject that have already been printed elsewhere singly should be united here into one collection. An older and similar interesting letter has been added as an Appendix.

F. H. REUSCH.

BONN, *June* 1890.

CONTENTS.

———o———

	PAGE

I. Considerations for the Bishops of the Council respecting the Question of Papal Infallibility, October 1869, . 1

II. A few Words on the Address presented to the Pope by certain Members of the Vatican Council urging him to declare his own Infallibility, Jan. 19th, 1870, . 33

III. The new Order of Business in the Council, and its Theological Significance, March 9th, 1870, . . 46

IV. Archbishop Gregory von Scherr of Munich-Freising to the Faculty of Theology in Munich, Oct. 20th, 1870, 65

V. Archbishop von Scherr to Döllinger, Jan. 4th, 1871, . 70

VI. Döllinger to Archbishop von Scherr, Jan. 29th, 1871, 74

VII. Archbishop von Scherr to Döllinger, Feb. 14th, 1871, . 78

VIII. Döllinger to Archbishop von Scherr, March 14th, 1871, 79

IX. Archbishop von Scherr to Döllinger, March 17th, 1871, 81

X. Döllinger to Archbishop von Scherr, March 28th, 1871, 82

XI. Archbishop von Scherr's Pastoral Letter, Palm Sunday, 1871, ... 105

XII. The Ordinariate of Munich-Freising to Döllinger, April 3rd, 1871, ... 111

XIII. The Ordinariate of Munich-Freising to Döllinger, April 17th, 1871, ... 113

XIV. The Ordinariate of Munich-Freising to the Parochial Office of St. Ludwig's Church, Munich, April 18th, 1871, ... 116

		PAGE
XV.	Döllinger to Widmann, Pastor at Todtnau, Oct. 18th, 1874,	117
XVI.	Döllinger to an old Catholic at Dortmund, June 23rd, 1878,	121
XVII.	Döllinger to Professor Michelis, May 1st, 1879,	122
XVIII.	Döllinger to Dr. Robert J. Nevin, Rector of the Anglo-American Church in Rome, May 4th, 1879,	124
XIX.	A Lady of High Rank to Döllinger, Feb. 15th and 28th, 1880,	126
XX.	Döllinger's Answer to a Lady, 1880,	130
XXI.	Bishop Hefele to Döllinger, June 10th, 1886,	135
XXII.	Archbishop Antonius von Steichele to Döllinger, 1878, 1879, 1886,	137
XXIII.	Döllinger to Archbishop von Steichele, March 1st, 1887,	141
XXIV.	Archbishop von Steichele to Döllinger, March 19th, 1887,	158
XXV.	Nuncio Ruffo Scilla to Döllinger, Oct. 1st, 1887,	159
XXVI.	Döllinger to Nuncio Ruffo Scilla, Oct. 12th, 1887,	161
XXVII.	Nuncio Ruffo Scilla to Döllinger, Oct. 14th, 1887,	169

APPENDIX.—Döllinger to a Dignitary of the Church, Feb. 7th, 1868, ... 172

I.

CONSIDERATIONS FOR THE BISHOPS OF THE COUNCIL RESPECTING THE QUESTION OF PAPAL INFALLIBILITY.

(October 1869.[1])

I.

IN past centuries, in opposition to projected innovations, the Catholic Church has always laid the greatest stress on the age and unchangeableness of her doctrines of faith. She has regarded it as a sacred duty, and, at the same time, as a high prerogative, that within her pale that only is taught and professed which has been believed everywhere, always, and of all men. Whenever it can be proved of a doctrine that it did not exist for several cen-

---

[1] Published by Manz of Munich without the author's name.

In a letter of November 25th, 1869, Döllinger says: "You will have received the pamphlet, 'Considerations,' etc. The sentences are for the most part set down as naked assertions. From Paris and elsewhere my attention has been called to the fact, that documentary evidence and historical criticism of what is here asserted so laconically, are indispensable. I am now occupied with this work, and in a short time shall publish a far more extensive supplement."

The supplement has not been published.

turies, that it was not the confession of the whole Church, or that it only took its rise at a certain period, and when this doctrine is not of logical necessity potentially contained as an undeniable sequence in other tenets of faith, then is this doctrine already condemned from the Catholic point of view; it bears the brand of illegitimacy on its brow, and neither may nor ever can be raised to the dignity of an axiom of faith.

This is just how the case of belief in papal infallibility stands. In the first place, it was altogether unknown in the Church for many centuries. It is here only necessary to call to mind the Eastern Church, which for a thousand years was united with the Western,—the Church by which all the Œcumenical Councils have been held, and by which especially the great mental work expended in the establishment of the dogmas of the Trinity and the Incarnation has been consummated,—a work which has gradually overcome all false doctrines, and created an independent ecclesiastical literature. But in this Church no voice has ever been heard to attribute dogmatic infallibility to the pope. Even Perrone has no testimony to cite from it.[1]

---

[1] Perrone, *Tractatus de locis Theologicis*, i. 510, ed. Lovan., appeals, it is true, to Origen, but with a gross mutilation of the passage and a distortion of the meaning. Just as dishonest is his appeal to Cyril of Alexandria, whose words he does not even think proper to quote.

Nor are there any witnesses to be found in the Western Church. Among the passages from the Latin Fathers, whom Perrone, Schrader, and other Jesuits quote, there is not a single one which even with some degree of clearness and distinctness attributes this high and divine prerogative to the popes, whereas three times the number of utterances of the Fathers can be brought forward, which expressly or in unmistakable hypotheses deny the popes such a privilege of infallibility, and refer the decision of what is an axiom of faith to the whole Church alone.

2.

It is not remarked of any single heretic of old that he began with, or was led up to, discarding the authority of the popes in matters of faith, a circumstance which can only be explained by the non-existence of such a high authority of the popes in which no one believed, and to which no one appealed, although the fact that Rome was the only See of the West founded by the apostles, and was the mother Church of so many local churches, invested it, it is true, with more importance and dignity in the West than it had in the East.

3.

In the writings of the ecclesiastical Fathers who treat of the rule of faith and the authority of the

Church, namely, in the writings of Tertullian, Cyprian, Augustine, Gennadius, and Vincent of Lerins, no reference is ever made to the judgment of the Romish See, or to the decisions of the popes, nor is it mentioned that there existed such a simple means of abruptly terminating doctrinal disputes as the consulting of the infallible papal dictum. All these Fathers only know of the traditions of the Church with the three conditions and marks of genuineness, viz. universality, antiquity, and general consent.

4.

Further, the doctrine of papal infallibility did not make its appearance in the Western Church until a very late period, and then only in consequence of a series of forgeries and inventions. It was not until towards the end of the thirteenth century that it was introduced into the School-theology by Thomas Aquinas, who was deceived by a new fiction; and theologians, in order to give it the appearance of a great ecclesiastical age, until far into the seventeenth century, made use partly of the forgeries of Pseudo-Isidore, and partly of those of others, as is recognisable in Bellarmine.

5.

To the adherents of the theory of infallibility, the history of the ancient Church in the first millennium must appear as an incomprehensible problem. The whole course, the long continuance, and the extensive complications of the great disputes on questions of dogma are for them inexplicable. For centuries the world has been drudging and slaving in order by long and toilsome circuitous routes to attain that which, if the popes are infallible, might have been gained by a far easier, shorter, and simpler method. As in their opinion the whole Church believed in the infallibility of the pope, a papal decision at the very beginning of a controversy must have obviated all further complications and disquietudes in the Church. Every Catholic submitted at once to the infallible dictum, and those who did not, either were expelled from the Church or they left it of their own accord. But in reality everything turned out quite different. The bishops were regularly summoned from all parts of the world. Long and difficult journeys necessitated a continued absence from their dioceses (an absence which was detrimental to the Church), and all this was done in order that in large assemblies exposed to divers dangers and temptations, they might pass resolutions which, after all, according to the views of the believers in infallibility, received all their power and authority from the assent of the pope. Nay, further, the popes themselves, as, for instance, Leo, have declared the necessity of a general Synod ; or, like Siricius, have declined a decision that was solicited of them, and referred it to a Council.

Cardinal Orsi, the most eminent defender of papal infallibility, has imputed the guilt of this "useless noise" of the Councils in the ancient Church to the Roman emperors. But these emperors by convoking the Councils were acting according to the advice of the bishops, and sometimes of the popes themselves; and however severely they have been blamed at times on account of the abuse of their power in ecclesiastical affairs, for a thousand years not a single word of censure was raised in condemnation of the emperors for attributing to the Councils the right of decision which belonged to the popes. The whole Christian world has held the decision in questions of faith by Councils to be the only legitimate course, and the one that corresponds to the principles of the Church.

6.

This is, however, no reason for asserting that the doctrine which transfers the infallibility of decision to the pope arose in the Church by means of a dogmatic process of development which fulfilled itself of internal necessity; for this new interpretation stands in reference to the old doctrine in no way as a rightly drawn sequence, but as a contradiction, as the negation of the earlier doctrine, and as the affirmation of one taking the place of the former, wholly different from it, and altogether incompatible with it.

The old doctrine says: The divine guidance and protection of the Church is shown by the fact that she cannot apostatise as a whole, and does not permit the doctrine entrusted to her to be contaminated or lost. It is then only to the whole Church, whether in her ordinary condition or in that of her representation by a Council, that this divine protection and enlightenment accrue, without which the promises of Christ would not be fulfilled, and which we designate the infallibility of decisions and of creed. The new school asserts the opposite to this, namely: It is not on the Church, but on one individual person, the pope, that infallibility is conferred, and without him she would be abandoned to error; he alone, as often as he speaks *ex cathedrâ* on matters of faith, receives a special divine illumination, which preserves him from every error; and it is from him that the Church first receives light and truth, and of these only as much as it pleases him to communicate to her.

7.

As an example and pattern, the Christian world had before it the earliest decision of a point of controversy in the first Church Assembly at Jerusalem. The most important question of that early period, the question as to the obligation of the Mosaic Law for the heathen Christians, was not decided at the dictation of Peter, but the apostles and elders at Jerusalem caused a prolonged discussion to be held in the presence of all believers; and then, though Peter was the first to give his opinion, the decree of the Assembly was formulated, not according to his declaration, but according to that of James, and was issued in the name of all.

8.

The decrees of the ancient Councils on questions of faith had full power, and were everywhere accepted without a confirmation of them by the pope being considered necessary, and even *before* such a confirmation had ensued. Of a papal confirmation of the Nicaean Decrees nothing is known, as indeed no appeal at all was made to the judgment of the Romish See during the whole Arian controversy. In the Second Synod, which was held at Constantinople in the year 381 A.D., the pope took no part, either in person or by delegates; nevertheless its decrees on the doctrine of the Holy Ghost were accepted at once by the whole Church, and were published as imperial laws by the Emperor Theodosius. Without the slightest initiative or assistance on the part of the pope, this Synod took the greatest, boldest, and most responsible step that can ever be ventured in the Church at all. By important additions it extended the Apostolic and Nicaean Creeds which were common to the whole Church. It did not take a single step towards effecting the sanction of the pope to this or indeed to any of its dogmatic decrees at all.[1] Hence it is that the popes for a considerable time refused to recognise this Council, or rather contradicted themselves in their utterances about its authority.

If the popes had already declared their opinion on a question of faith before the assembling of the Council, the papal document was first subjected to a detailed examination at the Council, and according to circumstances either sanctioned, as happened in the case of the dogmatic document of Leo to Flavian at Chalcedon, or rejected, as was the dogmatic letter of Honorius at the Sixth Council. Such an examination would have been an intolerable presumption had the popes been considered infallible.

10.

The prayer of Christ for Peter (Luke xxii. 32), that his faith might not fail, and the exhortation coupled with it, that, after his conversion, he should strengthen his brethren, is that passage of the Bible on which all infallibilists rest as confirming their theory, namely, by expounding it as a promise of infallibility

---

[1] The assertion of the Bishop of Grenoble, in his work, *Le Concile œcuménique*, 1869, that appeared recently, is unfounded.

for all popes in their intercourse with the "brethren," that is, with believers. But, in the *first* place, this interpretation contradicts the whole tradition of the ancient Church.

Second. It violates the oath taken by every bishop and priest.

Third. It is opposed to all rules of biblical exegesis, and hence no scientifically trained expositor will ever be able to advance or sanction it.

Fourth. It is refuted by a series of historical facts.

First, then, it contradicts the traditions of the Church. The Fathers, without exception, never understood it in this light. Not only in their biblical commentaries, but also in their other writings, where an opportunity of making use of this passage presented itself, we find no trace that even a single one of the old teachers of the Church found a promise of papal infallibility in the words of our Lord.

The ecclesiastical Fathers gave much and serious attention to the passage in Luke xxii. 32. We have the utterances of Saints Cyprian, Hilarius, and Chrysostom; of the two African Synods, those of Carthage and Milevi; of Augustine, Palladius, Leo, Theodoret, and several others, who have all recognised that it is here only a question of that individual virtue of faith which in the case of Peter and the apostles at the moment of a grievous temptation was to be weakened and obscured by the denial of the one, and by the fear and frailty of the others, which should not, however, completely die out in them, but should revive and become vigorous through the divine grace secured in the intercession of Christ. Christ prayed for Peter and the rest of the apostles that their faith in the Redeemer might be steadfast; it was in this faith that Peter was to strengthen the brethren after his own conversion. This is how the Fathers expound the passage, and this is what they teach.

The freedom from error of a doctrinal or judicial decision is something quite different from this. Such a decision or doctrinal statement, even with the firmest faith in Christ on the part of man, can nevertheless be erroneous, and has often been so, for no one will assert that all the African bishops, who, with Cyprian at their head, rejected the validity of baptism outside the Church, had therefore lost or never possessed faith in Christ. And *vice versâ*, a bishop who is inwardly an unbeliever, when questioned about a doctrine may be able to give a correct and orthodox decision.

The new interpretation then, that in this passage Christ was soliciting a dogmatic infallibility for the popes, does violence to the words and the context, and makes the Lord use the word "faith" in a sense which is quite unusual with Him, and which is unexampled in the New Testament.

For (*a*) the words, "when thou art converted," show that the words of Christ refer exclusively to the person of Peter, and it is inconceivable that every pope should, like Peter, fall away from the faith into unbelief, and then return again to the faith.

(*b*) The faith of which Christ speaks is the belief in His Messianic dignity and divine mission. Even supposing that in this passage there was the promise for every pope that he should always be kept in possession of this faith in Christ, it is still far from being a guarantee of infallibility for every single dictum on an article of ecclesiastical doctrine.

(*c*) The exhortation that Peter should strengthen his brethren by no means involves a promise that he would really do so in every single instance. It is a violent perversion to turn an admonition to duty into an infallible promise of the invariable fulfilment of that duty. Still less is any one justified in asserting that even if the exhortation of Christ to strengthen the brethren should at the same time refer to all the popes, the certainty is also involved that every one will do so in every instance.

The first who sought to turn this passage to account for the supposition of a special privilege herewith conferred on the Papal See, was Pope Agatho, in the year 680 A.D., when he feared the condemnation of his predecessor, Honorius, in Constantinople. But even he took care at the same time to excuse and to weaken his new and hitherto unheard of interpretation, by coupling with it the confession that at that time theological ignorance prevailed in Rome. Agatho's interpretation was then imputed to the earliest popes by Pseudo-Isidore, propagated and sanctioned by Gratian, and in this way gradually found acceptance, although constantly discarded by learned theologians and commentators.

But as it was not devised until so late a period, and as Pius IV.'s confession, which is given on oath and rests on the well-known canon of the Council of Trent, refers the Catholic Christian to the scriptural interpretation of the Fathers of the Church, *i.e.* of the first six centuries, every one who makes use of the passage as the basis of the doctrine of infallibility is, strictly speaking, guilty of perjury.

Finally, the facts of Church history show that, by this exhortation to Peter, Christ did not intend to confer the privilege of infallibility on all popes. For, if this were the case, we should have to be able to show that all popes for the last eighteen hundred years have always strengthened the brethren, and have never asserted or tolerated anything that was erroneous. But no man will seriously think of making such an assertion. It cannot be applied even to Peter himself, for he, far from strengthening the brethren in the faith at Antioch, rather perplexed them by his ὑπόκρισις, as Paul says. When

Zosimus approved a confession which denied original sin; when Liberius signed an Arian confession, and entered into Church fellowship with the Arians; when Honorius, according to the judgment of an Œcumenical Council, helped to spread the heterodoxy of Monotheletism—and how many other similar cases might still be quoted!—surely no one will be able to perceive in these instances a strengthening of the faith of the brethren.

II.

The testimony which the advocates of papal infallibility enforce with special predilection and confidence, the testimony which seems to express more than any other that can be derived from the Fathers, is the celebrated passage in the writings of St. Irenaeus. It is generally understood by them as though Irenaeus said that every individual Church is under the moral obligation of conforming to the Roman Church in doctrine. That this interpretation is erroneous, and imputes to Irenaeus a meaning foreign to his purpose, is clearly seen from the following statements:—

First. The sole fact on which the obligation of conforming to the Roman Church might be rested, namely, that a dogmatic privilege had been granted to Peter, and that this privilege passes on to his successors, of this Irenaeus does not utter a syllable. The prerogatives which he attributes to the Roman

Church are: extension, age, and foundation by Paul and Peter; whereas every adherent of the doctrine of infallibility always refers to Peter, and to him alone, as the sole bearer of it.

Second. According to Irenaeus, the necessity of conforming to the faith of the Roman Church results from the fact that believers from all parts (*undique*, πανταχόθεν) were compelled to go to Rome on account of her power and position in the world, consequently to enter into fellowship with that Church and by means of the touchstone of the tradition they had brought with them from their native towns and villages, to preserve in apostolic purity the Romish doctrine that was current there.

Irenaeus says: "The doctrine or tradition of the Church of Rome is very suitable in refuting heretics, because the Christians who flock together from all parts to this centre of the civilised world bring all their native beliefs with them, and preserve that Church from every deviation by this constant testimony, and by the consistency of their Asiatic, Egyptian, or Syrian traditions, which are thus always being compared with those of Rome." Irenaeus is here speaking, not of a "convenire *cum* ecclesiâ," but "*ad* ecclesiam." Two centuries later Gregory of Nazianzus speaks in the same terms of Constantinople, the new metropolis of the empire. "It is," he says, "the eye of the world. Everything that is noble flocks to it from all parts, and everything proceeds from it as from the common emporium of faith."[1] Thus the passage in Irenaeus is a speaking testimony, not for, but against papal infallibility; for Irenaeus knows nothing of a special privilege accorded to this Church or her bishop as a successor of Peter. He only knows that, by the concourse of Christians at Rome from all parts of the world, the genuine and universal tradition is preserved there. According to Irenaeus, the doctrine of the Roman Church is dependent on that of the rest of the Churches, *i.e.* on the Catholic Church; according to the Infallibilists, the doctrine of the whole Catholic Church is dependent on the particular Church of Rome.

The interpretation of Christ's words concerning an infallibility being guaranteed to the popes, stands, moreover, in contradiction to the limitations of this privilege as devised by its advocates. For if the scriptural origin of it is said to lie in the exhortation to the strengthening of the faith of others, a pope must be infallible even when he addresses himself only to a few brethren, only to two or three persons or to individual national churches; whereas Bellarmine, Perrone, and many others assert that the pope is not infallible

---

[1] *Opera*, ed. Benedictin. Paris 1778, i. 755. Symmachus, too, writes in the same strain: "In commune caput imperii (Rome) undique gentium convenitur."

until he addresses himself to the whole Catholic Church.

12.

In the controversy on the efficacy of baptism when administered by heretics, the dictum of Pope Stephen was discarded by a great part of the Church for more than sixty years. It is just in Rome itself that Cyprian, who with the whole African Church rejected Rome's decision, and died shortly afterwards, has nevertheless been held in veneration as a saint from the earliest times, so far were they, even in Rome at that period, from thinking of a privilege of infallibility. Subsequently Augustine, in oft-repeated utterances, justified the conduct of Cyprian and the African Church by showing that the declaration of Pope Stephen, however precisely it may have been worded, did not possess the power of obliging others to accept it, and that only the authority of a General Council, such as was held in the fourth century, had finally decided the question for the whole Church.

Cardinal Orsi can only get out of this difficulty by reproaching the celebrated ecclesiastical teacher with having set too high a value on the authority of a General Council, and too low an one on that of the pope. The question itself was one of the most important in the province of dogmatic teaching, for the whole doctrine of the conditions of the power and efficacy of the sacraments depended on the way in which it was answered.

13.

Pope Honorius was condemned at the Sixth General Synod on the charge of heresy. This condemnation was at once accepted by the whole Church without the slightest opposition. His successor sanctioned and signed it. No one, with the single exception of Anastasius Bibliothecarius, offered a word in his defence, and no one appealed to the infallibility of the popes in matters of faith. It is as clear as day that at that time the conception of such an infallibility was a thing totally unknown to the whole Christian world.

14.

The tenet that " the first See (the Roman) is not judged by any one," laid the foundation and prepared the way for the acceptance of a papal infallibility.

After a time the inference was drawn that he who can err in matters of faith, or fall into heresy, can also be judged, *i.e.* can be convicted of his error, by an ecclesiastical tribunal. Now, if the pope cannot be judged, this privilege must rest on another privilege, namely, on that of freedom from error. But the tenet itself was unknown to the early Church in the first five centuries, and it is only by inventions that it has been introduced into the Church. The great ecclesiastical Assemblies of Constance and Basel repeatedly rejected the tenet, that the first See is not judged by any one, and advanced the opposite doctrine, that the pope in matters of faith and the reformation of the Church is subject to a General Council, like every other Christian. Papal infallibility, as hitherto every adherent of this theory has admitted, is thus rejected ; for, did the pope really possess such a prerogative, the Council, as well as the whole Church, would have to submit itself to him and his decisions unconditionally.

16.

The Synod of Constance has been recognised generally by the whole Church and by the popes as a truly œcumenical one, and especially the decrees of its fourth and fifth session on the precedence of a Council over *every* pope, have been declared to be true and valid by a whole series of popes, by Martin V., Eugenius IV., Nicholas V., and Pius II. As they were proclaimed in the Synod without the slightest opposition, so also did no one in the whole Church raise his voice against them for over thirty years. It was not until a considerable time afterwards that Roman cardinals like Torquemada and Cajetan tried to make the authority and validity of these decrees doubtful. Lastly, when the theologians of the Jesuit order got the matter into their hands, they went so far as to discard the whole Council of Constance, and to strike it out of the list of Œcumenical Councils, and this, scarcely credible as it is, has been imitated but recently by some bishops; whereas Pope Martin V., in a special Bull, had declared such discarding of the Council to be a sign of heresy, and had ordered that every one who was suspected of heterodoxy should be specially asked if he believed that the Council of Constance was a general one, and if he assented to its decisions.[1]

If, then, the hypothesis of papal infallibility should be advanced to a doctrine of the whole Church, in the first place the whole Synod of Constance would have to be rejected, for the authority and validity of this great Synod stands and falls with the decrees of the fourth and fifth sitting. Secondly, the Synod of Basel, in its earlier period, as recognised by the Holy See before its removal to Ferrara, would also have to be discarded. Thirdly, the Bulls of the popes who have confirmed these decrees would have to be rejected. In this way the Catholic doctrine would be turned into a confused and contradictory chaos, which within the Church could only be asserted by force and violence, but outside her pale would be left without protection, and abandoned to the scorn

[1] Bull: Inter cunctas, post sess. 45 Concil. Constant.

and irrefutable reproaches of the anti-Roman theologians.

18.

Since the thirteenth century no principle or doctrine has been enforced with greater emphasis and more frequently repeated by the popes in circular letters, bulls, and enactments, than the doctrine that it is a divine commandment and a sacred duty for every monarch and every government to make use of the power that is given them for suppressing those who avow a different creed, and to permit no freedom in matters of faith and divine service. If, then, the dogma of papal infallibility is proclaimed, it is at the same time a declaration of the divine truth of the doctrine that Catholic princes and states, so far as they possess the necessary power, are also bound, as a matter of conscience, to tolerate no other but the Catholic confession, as far as possible to keep back from official positions those who differ from it, to undermine other Christian associations, and finally to extirpate them.

In a long series of bulls and decrees more than fifty popes established the institution of the Inquisition or the "Sacred Office." They restored it only a few years ago, after it had been suppressed in the Papal States by the Interregnum, and but recently they have again extolled it on the occasion of the canonisation of some inquisitors. For several centuries they enforced the rule that whoever persisted in differing from the Church doctrine in a single article, was to be punished by death; they sanctioned the principle that a relapsed heretic, *i.e.* one who has been convicted of differing for the second time from a doctrine of the Church, was to be executed, even if he recanted. Should the infallibility of the popes be proclaimed, it would self-evidently extend to the whole province of morals as well as to that of dogmas; it would be impossible to suppose that a pope had ever set up a principle that was reprehensible from a moral point of view, that he had ever issued an immoral decision, or instituted a proceeding that contradicted Christian ethics. No Catholic might, under these circumstances, either dare to say or think that the institution of the Inquisition was an error, or that the laws for it, given by the popes, had at times been immoral. Nevertheless, a glance at modern literature shows that nowadays, at all events outside Italy, no one dares any longer to defend the institution as it really was, or the laws and principles given and set up for it by the popes.

19.

If the infallibility of the popes be raised to a principle of faith, another doctrine that has been maintained by the popes since Gregory VII. will also receive the force of a dogma, namely, the doctrine of the submission of monarchs and kingdoms to the dominion of the Holy See, — a dominion which extends over secular and political matters. Every Catholic Christian is thus bound to believe, as a doctrine revealed of God, and which must be taught in every catechism, that the popes possess an absolute power over all princes and authorities, over all states and commonwealths, and that by their sovereign power they can interfere at discretion in all state affairs, depose princes, annul laws, and regulate war and peace.[1] Pope Boniface VIII.'s Bull, "Unam Sanctam," is a solemn dogmatic decision, addressed to the whole Church, and declares a belief in all this to be a condition of everlasting salvation. This doctrine was confirmed by Leo X. at the Synod of

---

[1] That the acceptance of this doctrine is indissolubly bound up with the acceptance of papal infallibility, has been long recognised by the defenders of the latter doctrine.

Thus Cardinal Baronius writes: "Haeresis errore notantur omnes, qui ab Ecclesiâ Romanâ, cathedrâ Petri, e duobus alterum gladium auferunt ac nisi spiritualem concedunt." *Annal. ad a.* 1053, 14, and again *a.* 1073, 13. Likewise Cardinal Bellarmine adversus Widdrington : "Illa sententia est haeretica, cujus contradictoria est de fide. Sed Pontificem habere potestatem deponendi principes est de fide ; est enim definitum et conclusum a S. Gregorio VII. in Concilio Romano, quod Papae liceat imperatores deponere, quod a fidelitate iniquorum subjectos potest absolvere." The Jesuit Lessius, *Pro potestate Summi Pontificis*, f. 396 : "Plane tenendum est, hanc doctrinam non esse ambiguam, ita ut utrumque opinari liceat, sed omnino certam, ita ut absque injuriâ fidei negari non possit. Primo igitur id probo, quia

the Lateran, and a whole series of papal decrees is founded upon it. It is true that by an artificial and violent interpretation the attempt has very recently been made to separate the main tenet, with a view to which very tenet the whole Bull, as is well known, was issued, from the rest of its contents, in which everything else stands only in the relation of a voucher of this tenet, and at the same time to assert that the pope may indeed in this tenet have fallen into error, but that this, in case his infallibility should be decided, in no way affects it in other respects. But with such a method of interpretation everything in ecclesiastical decisions would become uncertain, and it would lead to the ruin of all scientific dogmatic teaching.

20.

Further, the weighty and comprehensive dogmatic decree of Pope Eugenius IV. of the year 1439 A.D.

hae propositiones in terminis definitae sunt in Concilio Romano, quod Papae liceat imperatores deponere, quod a fidelitate iniquorum subditos potest absolvere. Atqui definitio facta a Summo Pontifice cum Synodo ad fidem pertinet." The most highly praised among the theologians of the Jesuit order, Suarez, *Defensio fidei cathol.* lib. 3, c. 22 et 23, lib. 6, c. 4, 6 : " Tam certum, Papam posse multis de causis principes poenis temporalibus coërcere vel punire, quam est certum, ecclesiam non posse in fide et moribus errare." Lib. 6, c. 8 : " Propositio haec : Papa habet potestatem ad deponendos reges haereticos et pertinaces, suove regno in rebus ad salutem animae pertinentibus perniciosos, inter dogmata fidei tenenda et credenda est. Nam continetur in verbis Christi Petro dictis, prout Ecclesia catholica illa intellexit, ut apertissime declaravit Bonifacius VIII. in Extrav. Unam Sanctam."

on the Incarnation and Sacraments will come into full force,—a doctrine in which the pope cannot have been in error, for he wished thereby to strengthen his brethren (principally the Armenian nation) in the faith, and lead them into the right way. But in this manner the whole doctrine of the Sacraments would be brought into the wildest confusion, and among other things, the fact would become manifest that there was no longer any true and valid ordination of priests and bishops in the whole Christian world, in the Eastern as well as in the Western Church.

Should then the papal infallibility be raised to a dogma, and therewith, as would follow naturally, the decree of Eugenius IV. be ratified as being free from error, those Protestant theologians who, like Pfaff, Mosheim, and many others, assert that there is no longer any true episcopal succession in the Catholic Church, would be right. But this would also mean the collapse of the whole authority of this approaching Council.

21.

The whole history of the Church shows, and, in conformity with this, all theologians teach, that the Church gives a more fixed and exact expression to a doctrine that has hitherto been believed and proclaimed, or that she establishes, limits, and defines that doctrine by a dogmatic decree, especially if it has been attacked from many sides, contested, suspected as an error, or misrepresented and distorted. This was just the position of papal infallibility at the time of the Synod of Trent. By all authors and adherents of Protestant teachings it was branded as an invention that lacked foundation, and as a device of later times. Moreover, the ecclesiastical theologians outside of Italy, who took under their especial protection all other doctrines which were assailed, were with few exceptions wont to abandon this one, either by their silence or in express words. It was accordingly strongly urged upon the Synod of Trent, if it regarded this doctrine as a part of the *depositum fidei*, and as being warranted by tradition, to raise it to an article of faith. Nevertheless, it was rejected by the Assembly, and the proposal that had already been made by the papal legates was withdrawn when they recognised that it was disapproved of by a number of the bishops.

22.

It is also of no slight importance that the doctrine of papal infallibility has only been spread by force and violence, and by the suppression of all who have taught in opposition to it. In Italy, Spain, and Portugal, the Inquisition made it impossible for any other doctrine to be presented either in books or from professorial chairs. A similar form of compulsion was exercised in the large ecclesiastical corporations, namely, the monastic orders. At the universities that were in the hands of the Jesuits it was never tolerated that the hypothesis of papal infallibility should even be doubted. All writings, too, which have put this doctrine to a scientific test and have proved its historical untenableness,[1] have been forbidden by the Index, and as far as possible suppressed. But where there is so complete a lack of freedom in teaching, there can be no question of a "consensus" of the Church, for the word in itself excludes every idea of compulsion.

23.

On comparing the theologians who profess their adherence to the one or the other doctrine, viz. to the infallibility of the Church or of the pope, it is undeniable that the preponderance of well-grounded learning, and especially of erudition in the Fathers and Church history, is to be found on the side of the adherents of the old doctrine, as every student of Church literature knows. Bossuet's work had such a convincing effect in Rome itself, that after its appearance, according to the testimony of Cardinal Orsi, the cause of papal infallibility was considered by many high authorities to be lost. The learned Maurines were all attached to the Gallican doctrine. The same

---

[1] With the exception of the works of Bossuet and of Cardinal La Luzerne.

thing is evident in Germany in modern times. It may be asserted that all theologians who combine a comprehensive historical knowledge with biblical and patristic erudition have rejected the new doctrine of papal infallibility.

Who then were the champions of this infallibility? Torquemada, Cajetan, Jacobazzi, Hosius, Polus, Baronius, Bellarmine, Aguirre, Pallavicini, Gotti, Orsi,—men who were either cardinals or who received the cardinal's hat in recognition of their services in this matter,—and along with these, monks of the great orders, whose generals resided in Rome; but, above all, Jesuits who have made it their chief aims, or rather their life's principle, to defend and carry out to a practical issue the unlimited power of the pope in every direction

24.

Now it happens that these theologians from the beginning have always rested their conclusions on false testimonies, fictions, and forgeries. The false decrees of Isidore, the invented testimonies of the Greek Fathers of the Church, which from the works of St. Thomas passed into the writings of the succeeding theologians and canonists, these along with several other spurious documents form the principal arguments for the champions of the theory of infallibility, namely, for Cardinals Torquemada and Cajetan, for the minorite

Capistrano, for Bellarmine, and the host of those who transcribed him. And so it went on. Nicholas Sanders, Roccaberti, and Aguirre, Vernant, the Jesuit General Thyrsus Gonzalez, the Jesuits Francis Turrianus, Alphonse Pisanus, Riccioli, and Raynaud ; then the theologians of the Roman Curia, Thomas and Camillo Campeggi, Bzovius, Vaira, Cardinal Sfondrati, Benettis, and numerous copyists of these men, without being disconcerted by the discovery of forgeries and inventions, erected their edifice of infallibility on this rotten and decaying foundation. Even at the present day the defenders of the doctrine will not desist from this argumentation, which is so ruinous to the honour and prestige of the Church, being impelled by the feeling that it would never have arisen were it not for these inventions. Thus Roskovany, the bishop of Neutra, in his great work on the pope, has again presented the long series of these fictions to the reader. The Jesuit Weninger, who, in publishing his book in New York and Cincinnati, seems to have aimed especially at the North American bishops and clergy, goes indeed so far as to give a purely fictitious account of the first General Council of Nicaea, in order to make the authority of the pope appear as the higher, and the one to be conformed to, as well as to cite as a witness for these untruths the Church historian Sozomenus, who, of course, says nothing about them. The Frenchman Bouix proceeds in a similar way in his recent work (*Tractatus de Papa*, 1869). He appeals to the spurious passage in St. Cyprian, and to such a late and ridiculous fiction as the so-called Arabian Canons of Nicaea. Similar things are to be found in the recent manifestoes of Archbishop Dechamps of Malines, as, for instance, the use he has made of a letter of St. Basil.

25.

Should the doctrine of papal infallibility really become an ecclesiastical dogma, it would present an incalculably weak point to the separated Churches—the Graeco-Russian and the Protestant. So far as can be foreseen, the whole controversy, as it has hitherto been carried on against the Catholic doctrine and Church, would concentrate itself more and more on this one doctrine, which would then have really become the "articulus stantis vel cadentis ecclesiae," and here the adversaries could borrow their most effective weapons and their most striking arguments from the very bosom of the Church herself, especially from the writings of her most eminent theologians. What reply will the champions of the Church be able to give when it is represented to them that for over eighteen hundred years this doctrine has been partly unknown and partly rejected and refuted by a great section of the Church, and that the most learned section; further, that the most respected and scientific corporation in the Church, the University of Paris, has been teaching the opposite for four hundred years; and, finally, what will they say when they are referred to the writings of Bossuet, Fleury, Natalis Alexander, and so many others! The whole doctrine of the Church, especially of the conditions and requirements of an ecclesiastical dogma, will gradually have to assume another form.

26.

One of the consequences which would of necessity follow the realisation of the theory of infallibility as an ecclesiastical dogma, would be the altogether incalculable enfeeblement of the prestige of the Church. For nothing can be more detrimental to the prestige of the Church in the eyes of all believers as well as of all strangers, than when it is proved that an ecclesiastical doctrine has been realised by means of, or, at least, under the effectual support of, premeditated innovations that have been long continued and firmly maintained. But this is, evidently and irrefutably the case with the doctrine of papal infallibility. The inventions by which this doctrine was prepared, recommended, finally introduced into the scholastic theology and the law books, extend from the sixth to the thirteenth century; and even St. Thomas Aquinas, whose authority has contributed so much towards the spreading and strengthening of the doctrine of infallibility, was deceived by fictitious testimonies of the Greek Church.[1]

[1] Compare what the Dominican Le Quien in the preface to his *Panoplia*, and de Rubeis in the introduction to the work, *Contra errores Graecorum*, in his edition of St. Thomas, say on the subject.

II.

A FEW WORDS ON THE ADDRESS PRESENTED TO THE POPE BY CERTAIN MEMBERS OF THE VATICAN COUNCIL, URGING HIM TO DECLARE HIS OWN INFALLIBILITY.

(January 19th, 1870.[1])

A REMARKABLE Address has been presented from the bosom of the Vatican Council to the pope begging him to take the necessary steps in order to have his own infallibility raised to an article of faith by the present assembly. A hundred and eighty millions of human beings—this is demanded by the bishops who have signed the Address—are, for the future, under threat of exclusion from the Church, of the withdrawal of the sacraments, and of everlasting damnation, to be compelled to believe that which the Church has hitherto never either believed or taught. "Has never believed," I say; for even those who have hitherto held papal infallibility to be true, could not *believe* it, taking this word in the Christian sense. Between faith—*fide divina*—and the intellectual acceptance of a doctrine that is considered to

[1] *Allgemeine Zeitung,* January 21st, 1870.

be probable, there is an immense difference. A Catholic can and may only *believe* that which is communicated and prescribed to him by the Church herself as a truth, which has been divinely revealed, which is one of the essentials of the doctrine of salvation, which is raised above all doubt, and on the confession of which alone depends his connection with the Church; while the opposite of it is not only not tolerated by the Church, but is rejected as manifest heterodoxy. As a matter of fact, then, no one, from the early beginnings of the Church to the present day, has believed in the infallibility of the pope, *i.e.* believed in it in the same way in which he believes in God, in Christ, and in the Trinity of the Father, Son, and Holy Ghost, etc.; but many have only conjectured, considered it probable, or, at most, humanly certain—*fide humana*—that this prerogative belongs to the pope. Consequently, the change in the faith and doctrine of the Church which the bishops, who have presented the Address, wish to see accomplished would be an event unique in the history of the Church. Nothing of the kind has happened during the last eighteen centuries. It is a Church revolution they desire, which is the more radical, because it is here a question of the foundation which is to support and preserve the religious faith of every individual, when a single man, the pope, is to take the place of the whole Church, which is universal in time and space. Hitherto the Catholic has said: "I believe this or that doctrine on the testimony of the whole Church of all times, because she has the promise that she shall exist for ever, and always remain in possession of the truth." But henceforth the Catholic will have to say: "I believe, because the pope, who has been declared infallible, commands it to be taught and believed; but that he is infallible, this I believe because he asserts it of himself, and not because at Rome, in 1870, 400 or 600 bishops resolved that the pope is infallible; for every bishop and every Council, apart from the pope, is subject to the possibility of error. Infallibility is the exclusive prerogative and possession of the pope. His testimony, the bishops, whether many or few, can neither strengthen nor weaken. Thus that resolution of the bishops has only so much power and authority as the pope gives it, by adopting it as his own. Everything thus resolves itself finally into the pope's testimony of himself, which is, indeed, a very simple matter. We need here only to remind ourselves that 1840 years ago One infinitely higher said of Himself, "If I bear witness of myself, my witness is not true" (John v. 31).

The Address gives occasion, especially, to the following considerations:—

First. It limits the infallibility of the pope to such dicta and decrees as are addressed by him to the whole body of believers, that is, for the instruction of the whole Catholic Church.

From this it would follow that, when the pope addressed himself to single persons, corporations, or to individual churches, he was always open to error; and yet for twelve or thirteen centuries the popes never realised the condition on which the freedom from error of their decisions or admonitions is supposed to depend. All manifestoes of the popes on questions of doctrine before the end of the thirteenth century were directed only to definite individuals, or to the bishops of a single country, etc. During the century of the union a universal decree of a pope was never once communicated to the Eastern Church as a body; it was only to individual patriarchs or to emperors—and that only at long intervals—that the popes directed any dogmatic writings.

Thus it is clear that the popes themselves, at least for a thousand years, had no idea of this condition to which the certainty and infallibility of their decisions are said to be subject, as indeed this assertion was not devised until a very late period, and was unknown to the Church before the year 1562 A.D. It was in this year that the theologian John Hessels of Louvain brought it forward for the first time. From him it was borrowed by Bellarmine, and supported by the spurious decretals of Isidore and the fictitious testimonies of St. Cyril. According to this theory, by prefixing a single word or by a simple endorsement, the popes might have conferred the highest prerogative of freedom from error to their dogmatic manifestoes; but they did not do so; they placed individuals and congregations in danger of falling a prey to error by the acceptance of their decisions, which were given without the guarantee of divine certainty.

Second. It is untrue that "according to the general and unchanged tradition of the Church the dogmatic decisions of the popes are unalterable." The opposite of this is manifest to every one. The Church has always first tested the dogmatic writings of the popes, and then, in consequence of this testing, either sanctioned them, as the Council of Chalcedon did the document of Leo, or rejected them as erroneous, as the Fifth Council (553 A.D.) did the "constitutum" of Vigilius, and the Sixth Council (681 A.D.) the letter of Honorius.

Third. It is not true that at the Second Council of Lyons (1274 A.D.) a confession of faith was accepted by the consent of the Greeks and Latins, a creed in which it is declared that "disputes on questions of faith must be settled by the decision of the pope." Neither the Greeks nor the Latins, *i.e.* those bishops of the Western Church who had assembled at Lyons, adopted this confession of faith, but the deceased Pope Clemens IV. had sent it to the Emperor Michael

Palaeologus as a condition of his admission to church-fellowship. Michael in the uncertain possession of the capital, that had been but recently reconquered and was now severely menaced by the Latin Emperor Baldwin and King Charles of Sicily, stood in urgent need of the pope, who alone was able to pacify his principal enemy. Hence it was that he consented to the conditions of submission to the Church as prescribed to him by the popes, although under the persistent contradiction of the Greek bishops and of the nation. Thus it was that he inserted the formula imposed upon him in the document which was read at the Council and confirmed by the logothete his ambassador. At home, in Constantinople, he himself declared that the three concessions he had made to the pope were illusory (*Pachymeres de Michaele Palaeol.* 5. 22). The assembled bishops have not been at all in a position to express an opinion on this formula.

Fourth. The decree of the Florentine Synod is here cited in a mutilated form. They have omitted precisely the principal passage, which was formulated as the result of long negotiations between the Greeks and Italians, and on which the greatest stress was laid because what preceded it was only to be understood according to the limitation therein contained, the passage, namely: "juxta eum modum, quo et in gestis et in sacris canonibus oecumenicorum conciliorum continetur." The pope and the cardinals persisted in requiring that as a more exact definition of how the primacy of the pope is to be understood, should be added, "juxta dicta Sanctorum." This was rejected by the Greeks with equal persistence. They well knew that among these "testimonies of the saints" there was a considerable number of extensive fictitious or spurious passages. As early as in the seventh sitting the Latin Archbishop Andreas, one of the speakers, had appealed to the notorious testimonies of Cyril, which, since Thomas Aquinas and Pope Urban IV. had been first cheated by them, had produced a great and lasting effect in the East, but were now rejected by the Greeks. The emperor remarked also that when one of the Fathers expressed himself in a complimentary style in a letter to the pope, no one could immediately deduce therefrom any rights and privileges. At last the Latins yielded. The "dicta Sanctorum" disappeared from the draft of the document, and in its place, as a standard and limit of the papal primacy, were set the negotiations of the Œcumenical Councils and the Holy Canons. Therewith, every thought of papal infallibility was excluded, since in the ancient Councils and in the pre-Isidore canons which were common to both Churches, not only is there nothing that would point to such a privilege, but the whole legislature of the ancient Church as well as the proceedings and history of the seven Œcumenical Councils—these were meant—clearly presume a state in which the highest authority of the doctrine only accrues to the Church as a body, but not to a single one of the five patriarchs. The pope was regarded as such by the Greeks. Moreover, Archbishop Bessarion had only shortly before in the name of all Greeks declared that the pope is inferior to the Council—consequently not infallible (Sess. ix. Concil. ed. Labbe, xiii. 150). It is thus a mutilation, which is tantamount to a forgery, to strike out of the decree of the Florentine Synod just the principal passage on which those for whom the decree was made laid the greatest stress. In the eyes of the Greeks the passage was so indispensable that they declared they would return home without effecting anything, if it were not inserted. By insisting, they also succeeded in having all the rights and privileges of the rest of the patriarchs reserved in the decree; as for the right of taking an independent part in the establishment of the Church doctrine which was common to all, and of not being obliged to submit simply to the claims of an infallible master, it had been declared at an earlier period by the popes themselves to belong to the patriarchs.

There is, it is true, another reason for the mutilation of the Florentine Decree that was committed by the compiler of the Address. Was he to give the Latin text in its original form corresponding to the Greek, as Flavius Blondus the secretary of Pope Eugenius IV. and the older theologians do, viz.: "quemadmodum et in actis conciliorum et in sacris canonibus continetur"? Or was he to adopt the forgery (first used by Abraham Bartholomaeus), according to which we are to read "etiam" instead of "et"?[1] By this "etiam" the sense of the decree is completely changed and the intention of the additional clause destroyed. But although it is a palpable forgery, it has passed over into the Council Collections and into the dogmatic manuals, and it is high time that this stone of offence for the Orientals be removed and the genuine text, namely, that which corresponds to the wording of the Greek, restored. But then, indeed, the decree would be no longer of any use for the purposes of the infallibilists, as De Marca, Archbishop of Paris, showed two hundred years ago (*Concord. Sacerd. et Imperii*, 3. 8). He is right in remarking: "Verba graeca in sincero sensu accepta

---

[1] On the authority of the papal secretary Flavio Biondo, who has correctly translated the Greek text, I assumed that the incorrect version of "quemadmodum etiam," which unmistakably alters the sense of the Greek, is a later change. But since then, from Frommann's statement in the *Allg. Zeitung*, as well as from the copy of the original document in the *Archivio Storico Italiano*, 1857, ii. p. 219, I have convinced myself that these words stood in the first Latin text, so that the Greek and Latin texts differed from each other from the very beginning. That the Greeks would not have accepted the text as it runs in the Latin version if they had known and understood it, is proved by the preceding transactions. (April 29th.)

modum exercitio potestatis pontificiae imponunt ei similem quem ecclesia Gallicana tuetur. At e contextus latini depravatâ lectione eruitur, plenam esse Papae potestatem idque probari actis conciliorum et canonibus."

The Address expresses special indignation (acerbissimi catholicae doctrinae impugnatores—blaterare non erubescunt) against those who do not regard the Florentine Synod to be œcumenical. Let the facts speak for themselves. The Synod was, as is well known, summoned with the express object of undermining the Council at Basel when the latter had begun to resolve upon several reforms that were troublesome to the Roman Curia. It was opened at Ferrara on the 9th of April 1438, but six months passed away without anything being done, so small was the number of the bishops who came to attend it. From the whole of northern Europe, at that time still thoroughly Catholic, from Germany, from the Scandinavian countries, from Poland, from Bohemia, from the France of that period, from Castile, Portugal, etc., not a single representative appeared at the Council. Nay, we may assert that nine-tenths of the Catholic world at that time did not take part in the Synod on principle, because they considered it, in the face of the Basel Assembly, to be illegal, and every one knew that for what was most urgent, viz. the reform of the Church, nothing would be done there. It was only with great difficulty that Eugenius was at last able to gather together an assembly of Italian bishops, about fifty, in addition to whom came some bishops sent by the Duke of Burgundy, some Provençals, and a few Spaniards,—in all there were the signatures of sixty-two bishops. The Greek prelates with their emperor, who saw that the fall of their empire was imminent, were attracted thither by the promise of money, ships, and soldiers. In addition to this, the pope had promised to bear the expenses of their sojourn at Ferrara and Florence, as well as those of their return journey. When they showed themselves unyielding, he withdrew his subsidies, so that they fell into terrible exigencies, and finally, compelled by the emperor and oppressed by hunger, they gave their signatures to things which almost all of them retracted afterwards. The opinion of Amyrutius, a Greek contemporary, which the Roman scholar Allatius quotes (*de perp. consens.* 3. 1, 4) was at that time the prevailing one among the Greeks. "Surely," he says, "no one will seriously call this Synod an œcumenical one, which has purchased articles of faith with money, and has only been able to pass its resolutions simoniacally by a prospect of financial and military assistance?" In France, before the Revolution, the Florentine Synod was rejected as not being genuine. This was declared by Cardinal Guise at the Council of Trent without meeting with the slightest opposition. The Portuguese theologian Payva de Andrada says on this point: "Florentinam (Synodum) sola Gallia — pro œcumenicâ nunquam habuit, quippe quam neque adire, dum agitaretur, neque admittere jam perfectam atque absolutam voluerit" (*Defens. fid. Trident.* pag. 431, ed. Colon. 1580).

The rest of the text of the Address is taken up with a detailed discussion to the effect that the advancement of the new article of faith is just at this time opportune, nay, of urgent necessity, because some persons who pretend to be Catholics have very recently contested this doctrine of papal infallibility. What the Address here partly expresses and partly presupposes as being well known (in Rome) is essentially the following: It would not have been absolutely necessary in itself to increase the number of dogmas by a new one, but the situation of affairs had assumed such a shape as to make it now unavoidable. Several years ago the order of Jesuits, supported by a following of similarly minded men, began an agitation simultaneously in Italy, France, Germany, and England in favour of the dogma that was to be made. A special religious society for the purpose of praying and working for the attainment of the new dogma has been founded and publicly announced by the Jesuits. Their principal organ, the *Civiltà*, published in Rome, has indicated the principal task of the Council beforehand, viz. the bestowal on the expectant world of this lacking article of faith. Their *Laacher Stimmen* and publications at Vienna have discussed the same subject in all its details and with untiring repetition. In this agitation it would have been the duty of all otherwise minded men to wait in respectful silence, to let the Jesuits and their adherents quietly go their way, and not to subject the arguments brought forward by them in numerous pamphlets to any test whatever. Unfortunately this has not been done. A few men have had the unheard of boldness to break the sacred silence, and to make known a different opinion. This offence can only be atoned for by an addition to the Creed, and by a change in the Catechism and in all manuals of religion.

III.

THE NEW ORDER OF BUSINESS IN THE COUNCIL, AND ITS THEOLOGICAL SIGNIFICANCE.

(March 9th, 1870.[1])

THE new order of business which has been imposed on the Council by the five cardinal legates, is entirely different from everything that has ever been customary at Councils, and it is at the same time determinative and decisive of the further course of this Assembly as well as of the numerous decrees that are to be brought into life by it. Hence it deserves our most careful attention. As regards its place in history, it is only necessary to mention briefly that a fixed order of business for the universal Councils of the ancient Church did not exist in the first millennium. It was only for provincial Councils held in Rome and Spain that there was a liturgical ceremonial.[2] Everything was brought forward in full assembly; every bishop had the right to move any resolutions he liked, while the presi-

---

[1] *Allgemeine Zeitung*, March 11th, 1870.
[2] Accepted by Pseudo-Isidore, and published by Mansi, *Concil. Coll.* i. 10.

dents, the secular who were sent by the emperor as well as the spiritual, kept order and conducted the proceedings in the simplest manner possible. The great Councils at Constance and Basel framed a special rule of order, as the division and voting according to nations was introduced. At Trent this arrangement was again forsaken; but the legates who presided came to an agreement with the bishops as to the order of business, and Cardinal del Monte took the vote on the subject, by which it was sanctioned *nemine contradicente*.[1] The present Roman Synod is thus the first in the history of the Church in which instructions as to procedure have been made to the assembled fathers beforehand, without their having any share whatever in the matter. The first Regolamento showed itself to be so obstructive and so unpractical that repeated petitions for its modification, and for permission to enjoy freer movement, were addressed to the pope by different parties of the episcopate. This was in vain. But after two months and a half the five legates themselves at last found that, if the Council was not to come to a standstill, changes and additions were urgently needed. In the new arrangement, however, no regard has been paid to the petitions of the bishops.

[1] Le Plat, *Monumenta*, iii. 418: "Dicant Patres, utrum hic modus procedendi eis placeat,"—whereupon the vote was taken.

In this arrangement there are two features which are especially prominent. In the first place, all power and influence on the course of the Council is laid in the hands of the presiding legates and of the deputations, so that the Council itself as opposed to these appears without power and will. In the second place, a simple majority is to decide all the most important questions of faith and of doctrine by standing up and remaining seated.

It is well known that during the two years which have preceded the opening of the Council, a number of treatises with the decrees and canons belonging to them have been elaborated. These are to be accepted by the Council, and then proclaimed by the pope "approbante Concilio" as laws and rules of doctrine and faith for the whole of Catholic Christendom. Altogether, there are fifty-one such schemes, of which hitherto only five have been discussed.

The method of procedure which is to take place at the deliberations and at the voting, is as follows:—

1. Several (ten) days before the deliberations, the scheme is distributed among the fathers of the Council, who can then make written memoranda, exceptions, and suggestions for improvement.

2. In this case they must at once bring forward a new wording of the article in question instead of the one they are contesting.

NEW ORDER OF BUSINESS IN THE COUNCIL.

3. Such suggestions are handed over by the secretary to the suitable deputation,—of these there are four,—which then, according to its discretion, makes use of them by reforming the scheme, if it consider it to be to the purpose, and by then giving notice to the Council of the proposed suggestions in a report which shall, however, only be a summary.

4. The presidents can submit every scheme to the deliberation of the Council, whether as a whole or as divided into paragraphs.

5. At the deliberations the presidents can interrupt any speaker if it appears to them that he is not keeping to the subject.

6. The bishops of the deputation can address the Council at any moment in order to reply to the bishops who contest the wording of the scheme.

7. Ten fathers are sufficient to move the closing of the discussion, which a simple majority shall then decide by standing up or remaining seated.

8. At the voting on the several parts of the scheme, the vote shall be taken by standing up or by remaining seated, so that the simple majority decides. The vote shall first be taken on the proposed alterations, and then on the text as brought forward by the deputation.

9. Hereupon the vote shall be taken on the whole scheme by calling out the individual names, to which each of the fathers shall answer "placet" or "non-

placet." Whether here, too, the simple majority of numbers shall rule, is not stated. But it appears as though this question must, according to analogy, be answered in the affirmative, for the whole scheme itself is, of course, only a piece or a part of a greater whole, and there is no reason why the greater part should be dealt with in a way different from the smaller. Were the principle of a simple majority to be here forsaken, it is just the more important and more deeply penetrating schemes that would probably be lost.

It is thus quite evident that a few parliamentary forms have been adopted in this order of business. But if in political assemblies there are certain arrangements similar to those given here, they generally serve to protect the minority from being compelled to follow the majority; while here they seem, on the contrary, to have been given for the purpose of making the majority still more powerful and irresistible, as is especially shown in the right that has been allowed them of cutting short the discussion as soon as they like. The effect of this will be all the more painful because, as is well known, even the possibility of communicating to the other members of the Council their opinions and ideas in print has not been given either to individuals or to whole groups of bishops.

In political assemblies resolutions can be passed, and even laws given, by a simple majority, because none of the succeeding parliaments and chambers is bound by the resolutions and laws of the earlier ones. Any assembly can at any time change or abrogate a statute of its predecessor. But the dogmatic resolutions of a Council, if it is really an œcumenical one, should be inviolably and irrevocably valid for all time.

At the voting that is now about to take place, the majority of the Council will presumably not be one that wavers like a wave of the sea ; it will not change with the resolutions that are to be passed, but will in its composition, with slight fluctuations in numbers, remain essentially the same. For it is well known that the division of the bishops into a majority and a minority, from the very beginning, as early as the election of the deputations, and even before a single vote had been taken, showed itself to be a sharp and decisive one. It was bound to be so, because in the question of papal infallibility a fundamental difference resting on matters of principle soon arose, and it was at once recognised that this question would form the chief business of the assembly, and that all other matters would be in abeyance to it. It is to be expected that the adherents of the theory of infallibility will also vote without any misgivings for the proposals as they come to them out of the hands of the deputations ; for, to them, all that proceeds from the Holy See is logically binding, and sufficient care has been taken that in the deputations, to which the most comprehensive and unquestionable power over all the proposals referring to improvements of the schemes has now been entrusted, only one opinion can make itself felt. A glimpse at the members of the most important deputation, *de fide*, will suffice. Prominent above all others we see here Cardoni of Rome, who, in the preparatory commission, had already recommended the dogma of papal infallibility in a special memorial, and had it accepted in his own commission. Beside him is the Jesuit Steins, and then the eloquent names of Dechamps of Malines, Spalding of Baltimore, Pie of Poitiers, Ledochowski, Hassun the Armenian, De Preux of Sitten; the Germans Martin, Senestrey, and Gasser of Brixen; two Spaniards, three South Americans, three Italians, an Irishman, and, finally, Simor, Regnier, and Schaepman.

For eighteen hundred years it has been held as a principle of the Church that decrees concerning faith and doctrine should be adopted by at least moral unanimity. This principle stands in the closest connection with the whole system of the Catholic Church. There is no known example of the introduction of a dogma after it having been resolved upon by a simple majority with the dissent of the minority.

In order to make this clear, I must solicit space for

a short theological discussion, which I hope, however, will be generally intelligible.

From the very beginning the Church has had entrusted to her a revealed doctrine which is to be preserved and administered by her.[1] She receives no new revelations, and she draws up no new articles of faith. As it is with the Church, so also is it with the General Council.[2] The Council is the representative, the sum of the whole Church; the bishops present are the ambassadors and deputies of the whole

---

[1] In the development of these questions, theology has attached itself to the work of Vincent of Lerins, viz. the *Commonitorium*, which is universally accepted as being classical and perfectly correct, and which appeared about the year 434 A.D. Hence it is to this work that I refer in the following paragraphs.

[2] Thus Fisher, bishop of Rochester, who sacrificed his life for the supremacy of the pope, writes in his polemical treatise against Luther (*Opera*, ed. Wirceburg. 1597, p. 592), appealing to the similar dictum of Duns Scotus: "In eorum (of the Council with the pope) arbitrio non est situm, ut quicquam tale vel non tale faciant, sed spiritu potius veritatis edocti id, quod reverâ pridem de substantiâ fidei fuerat, jam declarant, esse de substantiâ fidei." And the minorite Davenport, *Systema fidei*, p. 140: "Secundum receptam, tam veterum, quam modernorum doctorum sententiam ecclesia non potest agere ultra revelationes antiquas; nihil potest hodie declarari de fide, quod non habet talem identitatem cum prius revelatis. . . . Unde semper docet Scotus: Quod illae conclusiones solum possunt infallibiliter declarari et determinari per ecclesiam, quae sunt necessario inclusae in articulis creditis. Si igitur per accidens conjunguntur, vel si solum probabiliter sequuntur ex articulis, fidem non attingent per quascumque determinationes, quia concilia non possunt identificare, quae sunt ex objecto diversa, nec necessario inferre ea, quae solum apparenter seu probabiliter sunt inclusa in articulis creditis."

Church in the Catholic world; they have, in the name of the totality, to declare what this totality of the faithful thinks and believes on a religious question, and what it has received as tradition. They are thus to be regarded as procurators, who are not allowed on any conditions whatever to overstep the power entrusted to them.[1]

Were they to do so, the Church, whose representatives they are, would not confirm the doctrine and definition as set up by them, but would rather reject them as something foreign to her faithful conviction.

At the Council, therefore, the bishops are first of all witnesses; they express and state what they and their congregations have received and hitherto believed as doctrines of faith; but they are also judges, except that their judicial power over belief may not go beyond the range of their quality as witnesses, nay rather, that the latter constantly limits

---

[1] "Concilium non est ipsamet ecclesia, sed ipsam tantum repraesentat; . . . id est episcopi illi, qui concilio adsunt, legati mittuntur ab omnibus omnium gentium catholicarum ecclesiis, qui ex nomine totius universitatis declarent, quid ipsa universitas sentiat et quid traditum acceperit. Itaque ejusmodi legati omnium ecclesiarum sunt veluti procuratores, quibus nefas esset procurationem sibi creditam tantillum excedere. Unde constat, quod si quingenti episcopi, ut videre est in exemplis Ariminensis et Constantinopolitanae contra imagines coactae synodi, suam de fide communi declaranda procurationem tantillum excederent, universa ecclesia, cujus sunt tantummodo procuratores et simplex repraesentatio, definitionem factam ab illis ratam non haberet, imo repudiaret."—*Oeuvres de Fénelon*, Versailles 1820, ii. 361.

and circumscribes the former. As judges they have not first to make the law (the doctrine of faith), but only to interpret and apply it. They are subject to the Church's public right, in which they have no power to change anything. They exercise their judicial office, firstly, by examining the testimonies they themselves have borne, by comparing them with one another, and by considering the range of their efficacy; secondly, by declaring after a conscientious examination, whether the three indispensable conditions of universality, perpetuity, and consent (*ubique, semper, ab omnibus*) are fulfilled in a doctrine, *i.e.* whether the doctrine can be shown to all to be the universal doctrine of the whole Church, and a constituent part of the divine trust (*depositum*), and whether its confession can be imposed on every Christian.[1] Their examination has accordingly to stretch

---

[1] *E.g.* the Jesuit Bagot in his *Institutio theologica de verâ religione*, Paris 1645, p. 395: "Universitas sine duabus aliis, nimirum antiquitate et consensione, stare non potest. Quod autem triplici illâ probatione confirmatur, est haud dubie ecclesiasticum et catholicum. Quod si universitatis nota deficit et nova aliqua quaestio exoritur, novaque contagio ecclesiam commaculare incipit, tunc hac universitate praesentium ecclesiarum deficiente recurrendum est ad antiquitatem. Notat enim Vincentius, posse aliquam haereseos contagionem occupare multas ecclesias, sicut constat de Ariana, adeo ut aliquando plures ecclesiae et episcopi diversarum nationum Ariani quam catholici reperirentur. Et quantumvis doctrina aliqua latissime pateat, si tamen novam esse constat, haud dubie erronea est, nec enim est apostolica, nec per successionem et traditionem ad nos usque pervenit. Deinde, ut notat idem Vincentius, antiquitas non potest jam seduci.

over the past as well as the present. All arbitrariness and every opinion that is simply subjective is thus excluded from the duty of the bishops at Councils. It would be outrageous and ruinous there; for as the Church does not receive any new revelations, and makes no new articles of faith, a Council neither can nor may change the substance of the faith, nor take anything away from it, nor add anything to it. Thus a Council only makes dogmatical decrees on things which were already universally believed in the Church as being testified by the Scriptures and by tradition,[1] or which are contained as evident and clear deductions in the principles that have been already believed and taught. But if an opinion has for centuries constantly met with contradiction, has been contested

Verum enimvero quia et ipse error antiquus esse potest, idcirco, cum consulitur vetustas, in eâ quaerenda est consensio."

[1] Thus Vincent writes: "Hoc semper *nec quidquam aliud* conciliorum decretis catholica perfecit ecclesia, nisi ut quod a majoribus solâ traditione susceperat, hoc deinde posteris per scripturae chirographum consignaret, *Commonit.*" cap. 32. The Tridentine theologian Vega, in Davenport, p. 9, says: "Concilia generalia hoc tantum habent, ut veritates jam alias, vel in seipsis, vel in suis principiis a Deo ecclesiae vel SS. Patribus revelatas, vel per scripturas vel traditionem prophetarum et apostolorum, tum declarent, tum confirment et suâ autoritate claras et apertas et absque ullâ ambiguitate ab omnibus catholicis tenendas tradant. Addit: et ad hoc dico; praesentiâ Spiritus sancti illustrantur, primo ut infallibiles declarent veritates ecclesiae revelatas, et secundo, ut ad terminanda dubia in ecclesiâ suborta extirpandosque errores et abusus infallibiliter etiam ex revelatis colligant populo christiano credenda et usurpanda in fide et moribus."

with all the weapons theology can produce, and accordingly has, to say the least, always been uncertain, it can never, not even by a Council, be raised to a certainty, *i.e.* to the dignity of a divinely revealed doctrine. Hence the usual exclamation of the Fathers at the Councils after the acceptance and proclamation of a dogmatic decree: *Hacc fides patrum.*

Should, for example, the infallibility of a single individual be put in the place of the freedom from error of the whole Church as formerly believed and taught, this is no development nor explanation of what was hitherto implicitly believed, nor is it a deduction that follows with logical accuracy, but simply the very opposite of the earlier doctrine, which thereby would be subverted. Just as it would be in political life no development, but simply a subversion and a revolution, if a hitherto free community were suddenly put under the yoke of an absolute monarch.

The time during which an Œcumenical Council deliberates on the faith of Christians has thus always been a time of the most stirring revival of the religious consciousness, a time of bearing testimony and of making open declarations on the part of all faithful sons of the Church, laity as well as clergy. As the history of the Church shows, it was generally believed that just such utterances would lighten the task of the Council without disturbing or hindering the fathers. Every one, also the layman, can and may bear testimony, express his wishes, and point out the needs of the Church.[1]

It is most especially when it is a question of the introduction of a new dogma, which, though demanded perhaps from one quarter, is foreign to the conscience of the faithful, and appears to them as an innovation, that the protest raised by the laity is as just as it is necessary, an indispensable testimony of their adherence to the faith that has been delivered to them, and they fulfil thereby a duty towards the Church.

Moreover, at the Council itself the opposition a number of bishops raise against an opinion that is to be proclaimed as a dogma, is a proof that in the local Churches represented by them this opinion has not been believed to be true or divinely revealed,

---

[1] As Cardinal Reginald Pole, one of the presidents of the Council of Trent, says in his book, *De Concilio*, 1562, fol. 11 : "Patet quidem locus omnibus et singulis exponendi, si quid vel sibi vel ecclesiae opus esse censeant; sed decernendi non omnibus patet, verum iis tantum, quibus rectionem animarum ipse unicus pastor et rector dedit."—Pope Nicholas I. remarks that the emperors took part in the Councils when questions of faith were discussed. "Ubinam legistis, imperatores antecessores vestros synodalibus conventibus interfuisse, nisi forsitan in quibus de fide tractatum est, quae universitatis est, quae omnium communis est, quae non solum ad clericos, verum etiam ad laicos et ad omnes omnino pertinent christianos?" This passage was also admitted into Gratian's decree.

and that even now it is not considered to be so. But this is decisive enough to prove that this doctrine or opinion is wanting in the three essential requirements of universality, perpetuity, and consent, that it accordingly may not be forced upon the whole Church as a divine revelation.

Hence it is that in the Church it has always been regarded as necessary, that as soon as a somewhat considerable number of bishops oppose a decree which has been proposed or intended by the majority, this decree is laid aside and the definition suppressed. The true catholicity of a doctrine must be clear and undoubted; but it is not so as soon as the testimony of even only a minority supplies the proof that whole divisions of the Church neither believe nor confess this doctrine.

Hence, at every Council the principal question was: Have the decrees of faith been sanctioned by all the members? This was already the case at the first General Council of Nicaea, where, out of 318 bishops, finally only two refused their signatures. At Chalcedon they hesitated with the decisions, and kept entering repeatedly into new discussions, until at last all scruples were removed, which had at first been cherished, especially by the bishops from Illyria and Palestine, against the letter of Leo. Even before the Emperor Marcian dismissed the Synod, he pressed for a declaration whether all the bishops (there were above six hundred of them) really gave their consent to the definition of faith. An answer in the affirmative was then readily given by all, whereupon Pope Leo himself thanked God that his letter had "in the face of all doubts and scruples been at last confirmed by the irrefutable consent of the whole episcopate." In the same way at the Sixth General Council, the bishops, on being questioned by the emperor, gave assurance that the dogmatic decision had been made with the consent of all. The same thing occurred at the Seventh Council in the year 787 A.D., and further Charlemagne announced to the Spanish bishops from the Council of Frankfort, 794 A.D., that all had taken place "quatenus sancta omnium unanimitas decerneret," etc.

At Trent, Pope Pius IV. gave the legates the hint not to let anything be decided that was not agreeable to all the fathers. One of the theologians who were present, Payva de Andrada, reports that several times a decree was left undecided for weeks and months because some few bishops opposed it or had scruples about it, and that the decree was not published until, after long and careful deliberation, the unanimity of the fathers was at last attained. Payva quotes several examples of this.[1] Bossuet too, discussing the in-

---

[1] *Defensio fidei Tridentinae*, f. 17: "Cum quindecim fere aut viginti dubitare se ajebant, ne vero quicquam praeter conciliorum vetustum morem concluderetur, horum paucorum dubitatio plurimorum impetum

NEW ORDER OF BUSINESS IN THE COUNCIL. 61

structions of Pius IV., remarks that this was an excellent rule for separating the truth from what is doubtful.

All theologians make it a condition of the œcumenical character of a Council that perfect freedom should prevail at it—freedom of speech and freedom of voting. "No one may be rejected," says Tournely, "who wishes to be heard." It is not simply physical force that would make the resolutions of a Council powerless and worthless. Freedom, that vital air of a real Council, is also destroyed by the very manifold forms in which moral force makes its appearance, or man willingly allows himself to be enslaved (*e.g.* by the different kinds of simony), whereby the legitimacy of the Council becomes null and void. Tournely names as passions that work effectually at synods, and that render the freedom of the Council null and void, fear, desire for office, avarice, and covetousness.[1]

When the great defection took place at Seleucia, and at the same time at Rimini, and when close upon six hundred bishops denied and abandoned the common faith, what won them over was "a weakness of mind and shyness of a tedious journey"

retardavit atque effecit, ut res in aliam sessionem dilata, omnium fere calculis tandem definiretur." Compare also what follows. It is clear that at Trent the conviction prevailed that everything must be done and decided in the same way as at the old Councils—at all events that the essential form of them should be retained.

[1] *De ecclesiâ*, i. 384.

("partim imbecillitate ingenii, partim taedio peregrinationis evicti," Sulp. Sever. 2. 43).

The mere fact then of an episcopal assembly, however numerous, is a long way from being a proof of the real œcumenical character of a Council, or as the theologians express themselves, *e.g.* Tournely, it may possibly be œcumenical according to its vocation, but whether it is so according to its course and issue cannot be decided by the Council itself, for it cannot bear witness of itself. It is still necessary that the authority which stands even above every Council, or the testimony of the whole Church, should come forward to decide and confirm. The Councils as such have no promise. Even in the commonly quoted words of our Lord of the "two or three," all depends on the "gathered together in His name," and this involves, as all theologians accept, several conditions which Tournely for instance specifies.[1]

---

[1] "Quaeres: quibus conditionibus promisit Christus se conciliis adfuturum? Resp. Ista generali: si in nomine suo congregata fuerint; hoc est servatâ suffragiorum libertate, invocato coelesti auxilio, adhibitâ humanâ industriâ et diligentiâ in conquirendâ veritate. . . . Deus scilicet, qui omnia suaviter disponit ac moderatur, viâ supernaturali apertâ et manifestâ non adest conciliis, sed occultâ Spiritus subministratione. (Deus) permittit, episcopos omnibus humanae infirmitatis periculis subjacere et aliquando succumbere; neque enim unquam promisit, se a conciliis ejusmodi pericula certo semper propulsaturum, sed hoc unum, se iis semper adfuturum, qui in suo nomine congregarentur. Congregari autem in suo nomine censentur, quoties eas observant leges et conditiones, quas voluit observari." Tournely.

But the Church has her promises, and she must first convince herself or possess the certainty that physical or moral force, fear, passions, and arts of seduction—such as were effectual at Rimini, and even often at other times too—have not become too powerful at the Council, and that accordingly true liberty reigned there. In this sense Bossuet says of an Œcumenical Council that a great many bishops must be there, and from different countries, and that the consent of the remaining bishops must be so manifest that one might clearly see nothing else had occurred there except the bringing together of the views of the whole world.[1] Should it then be shown that at the Council " the views of the

Praelectiones theologicae de Deo et divinis attributis, i. 265. Tournely continues the same thought in his *Praelectiones theologicae de ecclesia Christi*, i. 384: "(Deus) episcopos permittit omnibus humanae infirmitatis periculis obnoxios esse, metus scilicet, ambitionis, avaritiae, cupiditatis," etc.

[1] " Et que les autres consentent si évidemment à leur assemblée, qu'il sera clair, qu'on n'y ait fait qu'apporter le sentiment de toute la terre" (*Histoire des variations*, i. 15, n. 1000). And hence it is that Pope Gelasius demands of a *bene gesta synodus*, not only that it has made its decisions according to the Scriptures and tradition and ecclesiastical rules, but also that it has been accepted by the whole Church: "quam cuncta recepit ecclesia" (Epist. 13 in Labbe, Concil. IV., 1200 and 1203); and Nicole remarks against the Calvinists: "Ils ont une marque évidente que le concile, qui se dit universel, doit être reçu pour tel, dans l'acceptation qu'en fait l'Église" (*Prétendus Réformés convaincus de schisme*, 2. 7, p. 289). The Church gives the Councils testimony (not first authority) as she gives the single books of the Bible testimony by her biblical canon, while, of course, their internal authority does not proceed from the Church. She is also there as *testis, non auctor fidei*.

whole Catholic world have not been brought together," but that rather the resolutions of majorities have been passed, which stand in contradiction to the belief of a considerable part of the Church, it is certain that the following questions would then arise in the Catholic world: Have our bishops borne true witness of the belief of their dioceses? If not, have they been really free? Or how comes it that their testimony has not been considered, and that they have been overruled by the majority? Ensuing events in the Church will be conditioned by the answers given to these questions. Hence it is that in the whole Church the fullest publicity has always been afforded as appertaining to a Council: for it is a matter of great concern to the whole Christian world, not only to know *that* something will be resolved upon there, but also to know *how* it will be resolved upon. Everything depends finally on this *how*, as is proved by the memorable years 359, 449, 754 A.D. etc. Touching the silence that was imposed by force, an appeal ought not to have been made to the Council of Trent; for, first, only an exhortation was given there, and, second, the reminder only effected the giving notice of drafts, a thing which at the present day would no longer be possible on account of the position of the press, but at that time at a distance they were confounded with genuine decrees.

IV.

ARCHBISHOP GREGORY VON SCHERR OF MUNICH-FREISING TO THE FACULTY OF THEOLOGY IN MUNICH.

(October 20th, 1870.[1])

To the Reverend Faculty of Theology.

In addressing the present letter to the Theological Faculty of the Ludwig-Maximilian University, I am only following the voice of my duty as bishop, in order, as far as in me lies, to remove the harassing doubts and anxious uneasiness which prevail in the widest circles in reference to the position which this Theological Faculty intends to assume towards the General Vatican Council and the Resolutions hitherto adopted by it.

To enter into an explanation of how these doubts and this uneasiness have arisen, is, on the one hand, unnecessary, because the events connected with them are everywhere well known, and consequently are

[1] Nos. iv.–xiv. are reprinted from the *Documents of the Ordinariate of the Archbishopric of Munich-Freising concerning the General Vatican Council*, Ratisbon 1871.

certainly not concealed from the Theological Faculty itself; on the other hand, such an explanation would involve too much pain for me, who from the beginning of my episcopal office up to the present day have been disposed to this venerable corporation with special feelings of honour, esteem, and love, as is well known to the corporation itself.

Thus, then, though I willingly let the past rest, henceforth I can no longer admit that there exists any well-founded doubt about the dogmatical position of even a single one of its members.

As you certainly do not stand in need of any dogmatic teaching from me, I shall here limit myself to the following. Hitherto the Resolutions of the General Vatican Council have been made with all those formalities that are requisite for their validity. This is attested by the bishops of the so-called Minority as well as by the rest. As a matter of fact, up to the present not a single Catholic bishop has raised his voice against the legality of the Resolutions that have been passed. On the contrary, by far the greatest proportion have made known their submission to them in some unambiguous way.

During the deliberations I gave utterance to my own opinion with all the positiveness of a conviction that had been arrived at after mature consideration;

but at the same time I never intended to retain this conviction of mine if the decision should turn out differently. After having thus fulfilled my first duty, I did not hesitate one moment to submit myself unconditionally to the legally made Resolutions. From you, reverend gentlemen, where it is a question of a principle of the Catholic Faith, I shall certainly not have to fear the thoughtless reproach of a change of conviction.

Seeing, then, that the position of things is now incontrovertibly clear, it is impossible for it to be a matter of indifference to me what position the venerable Theological Faculty and its individual members assume in reference to it. However gladly I should grant every one else time to fight out to the end the severe internal contest which the conflict between the view he has hitherto held and the solemn decisions of the teaching Church cost him, this is no longer possible in the case of public teachers of theology who in a few days will be again entering upon their duties. It is impossible for me in silence to allow the sacred science to be taught in my diocese by any one of whom I am not certain that he teaches what the Catholic Church has expressly declared, without exception and without reserve. It is impossible for me to let my candidates for the priesthood stand in danger of being instructed in a different way from that which is in accordance with the will of the Catholic Church. Finally, to tell you the whole truth, I cannot bear the thought of the venerable Theological Faculty, the pearl of my diocese, staining her glorious history and the decided great merits of many of her present members by an unjustifiable and fruitless isolated position in the Church. Therefore, reverend gentlemen, full of fatherly love, I beg you, by invocation of the divine assistance and in common deliberation together, to consider your duties towards the decisions of the General Vatican Council, and to express your unanimous opinion to me clearly and distinctly as to how you intend to meet them.

In conclusion, I must also offer the following for your consideration. It is well known to you that hitherto I have at all times stood faithfully by you, and that in opposition to all kinds of trials I have always protected my Professors of Theology with the shield of my pastoral dignity. Nor in this have I imitated the examples of other bishops towards you. It is perhaps less known to you that during the past summer in an interview with the Holy Father himself, I represented and defended you zealously and steadfastly. Under quite different conditions, I should perhaps not be able to do so again. May you therefore preserve me from the pain, which would certainly be the greatest during my episcopal office, namely, that of being obliged to employ against you the severity of my pastoral duty.

In fatherly love, sincere respect, and hearty devotion, yours faithfully,

✠ GREGORIUS,
Archbishop of Munich-Freising.

MUNICH, *October* 20*th*, 1870.

V.

ARCHBISHOP VON SCHERR TO DÖLLINGER.

(January 4th, 1871.)

REVEREND SIR, — It was with the greatest pain that I missed the name of the venerable senior of our Theological Faculty among those of its members who, on the 29th November last, in a satisfactory manner answered my letter of the 20th of the previous October, with which your Reverence is also fully acquainted.

Since then a considerable interval of time has elapsed, during which I have been in vain expecting an answer and declaration such, as it appears to me, would be meet for you also to give concerning your position to the Œcumenical Vatican Council and its Resolutions up to the present.

Thus, at last, after long hesitation, the significance of which your Reverence will know how to value, I now see myself compelled to request and formally challenge you to an open expression of your opinion on this subject.

I can well imagine what renders a candid declaration of your position to the matter in question so very difficult.

Your glorious past, which has been filled with meritorious deeds on behalf of Catholic science, of our future Catholic clergy, and of the representation of the Catholic Church in public life, acts as a powerful barrier to a breach with the Church to which you have belonged all your life.

On the other hand, to that side which in Germany occasioned the well-known agitations against the Council both before and during its deliberations, and which always, whether rightly or wrongly, appealed to your name, you seem to have made concessions of such a kind that it will now cost you a severe struggle to renounce them.

And yet one would think it were easier for you to separate yourself from associates that have been but lately gained, than from the long period of your life which has attached such merited glory to your name, and, at the same time, to break altogether with the Catholic Church.

Cast, I beg you, a glance at the daily literary effusions of that party which is making fraudulent use of the dogma of infallibility of the highest ecclesiastical office in order to degrade the Catholic Church herself in the eyes of the public, and which, though, of course, wrongly, constantly appeals to your authority, and then address to yourself the following question: "Into what kind of company have I fallen?"

Make, then, a retrospect of the whole great domain of ecclesiastical history, and see if you can discover even of one who could tear himself away from the Holy Roman See, the *cathedra Petri*, without, at the same time, falling away from the unity of the Catholic Church.

Consider, further, in serious thought, the final issue of all those who have persisted in offering resistance to the Holy Church.

In conclusion, take to heart the great responsibility you will have to bear before the judgment-seat of God for all those who allow themselves to be detained still longer in their isolation by your example.

When I, finally, pray you to remove from the paternal heart of your bishop all the grief that at present already troubles it on your account, and which must now either come to an end or increase until it becomes unbearable, you will feel yourself compelled to ascribe to my love for you this appeal of mine to your Catholic heart.

The esteem in which I have held you at all times has been changed into a close attachment since I entered on my pastoral office, which gave you to me as a specially precious treasure. I can declare it as the truth, of which you also have received proofs, that

I regarded you, not as my son, but as my friend and brother.

I pray and conjure you, therefore, cease from assisting to cause the unity and unanimity among the members of the one Church to suffer harm longer, and with an heroic resolution, by a public Catholic confession, break the ban which, up to the present hour, still holds many an honest Catholic in its grasp.

It is still impossible for me to believe that, instead of giving my pastoral heart this joy, you will challenge the authority of your bishop, which, however, must and will most certainly exercise its inalienable rights, if hopeful patience must see itself deceived at last.— In sincere esteem and veneration, yours faithfully,

✠ GREGORIUS,
Archbishop of Munich-Freising.

MUNICH, *Jan. 4th*, 1871.

VI.

DÖLLINGER TO ARCHBISHOP VON SCHERR.

(January 29th, 1871.)

MY LORD ARCHBISHOP,—The letter which your Grace has addressed to me, and in which you call upon me to declare my submission to the Decrees of Faith proclaimed at Rome on the 18th July, did not surprise me. After the Resolution which your Grace in conjunction with other bishops passed at Fulda, it was only what I had to expect.

But it would not now be feasible for me to give a simple and unsubstantiated declaration of consent or submission, were it only because I have repeatedly asserted the opposite doctrine in public ever since the beginning of the Vatican Synod, and have supported my views by many evidences. I should have at the same time—indeed this would be the only way open for me—to refute myself, and publicly to bring forward proof that the doctrine I taught, as well formerly as especially very recently, was a false and perverted one. Were I to do this, nobody, at all events no one who knows anything of my writings and public declarations, would believe in the sincerity of my submission. The whole world, abroad as well as at home (with the exception, perhaps, of a few nuns), would brand me as a wicked, unprincipled hypocrite, who was denying his own convictions from fear and personal interest.

Conscious of the painful position in which I am placed, and of the responsibility with which I am burdened, I have for some weeks been making the great question of the nature and extent of the papal authority and its relation to the Church the subject of renewed study and of a most careful and searching investigation. I am reading and proving everything that has recently appeared on the Roman side in defence of the Decrees and of the doctrine contained in them, partly in Italy, partly in France, England, and Germany, as far as it is within my reach. Should I succeed in gaining the conviction that this doctrine is the true one as warranted by the Scriptures and by tradition, and that I, who have hitherto believed the opposite, as the large majority of German theologians have done, am in error, I shall then not hesitate to confess this before the world without reservation and without any attempt at palliation; I shall then, as far as God gives me strength of body and mind, go still further—I shall endeavour in some degree to redress the injury which may have accrued to the Church by the books I have written and by the lectures I have delivered in the opposite sense during the last forty-seven years, and I shall do this by refuting myself, and by disclosing my own faults and erroneous views. I am fully aware that a priest must also be ready to make this noblest and most difficult of all sacrifices to the Church, namely, the sacrifice of his good reputation and honour before his fellow-men. Yet this is to be done only on one condition, namely, that he is also really convinced of the truth of what he is to confess anew, and of the falseness of what he has previously taught; for without this conviction a submission of this kind would, of course, be a grievous sin and a gross lie, and I am quite certain that your Grace does not intend to drive me to such an extremity by your challenge. Your challenge can only bear this interpretation: "Take pains and do all you can to procure for yourself the same conviction as I have now." This is just what I am doing as conscientiously as I can. I am invoking God to give me light, I am investigating and proving as well as I know how; but on account of the extensiveness of the subject and materials to be inquired into, this is a task for which a longer time is requisite, and I therefore beg you to grant it me and still to have patience with the old man.

There still remains for me to express my thanks for the friendly and humane strain which was maintained in the greater part of the letter. The conclusion is indeed severe and menacing, but — I know the individuals and influences at work in this matter, and it is only what I was expecting.—In the highest esteem, I remain, your most obedient servant,

J. V. DÖLLINGER.

MUNICH, *January* 29*th*, 1871.

VII.

ARCHBISHOP VON SCHERR TO DÖLLINGER.

(February 14th, 1871.)

REVEREND SIR,—It is to my very great sorrow that your letter of the 29th ult. does not contain the satisfying declaration about your position in regard to the General Vatican Council and its Resolutions up to the present, which I had confidently expected, and which I must demand in accordance with my pastoral duty. I see myself, therefore, compelled to inform you that I shall look for a final declaration by the 15th March, and that from this date I have definitely resolved to take the further steps which my office as bishop requires of me.

Still indulging the hope that I shall be spared the necessity of any disagreeable measures,—I remain, yours faithfully,

✠ GREGORIUS,
Archbishop of Munich-Freising.

MUNICH, *February 14th*, 1871.

VIII.

DÖLLINGER TO ARCHBISHOP VON SCHERR.

(March 14th, 1871.)

MY LORD ARCHBISHOP,—The term your Grace has appointed me in reference to a declaration on the Vatican Decrees expires to-morrow. I see myself, however, compelled to petition your Grace kindly to prolong the time for another twelve or fourteen days. During the last few weeks so many documents from far and near, so many counsels, warnings, and urgent remonstrances have been addressed to me, high and low have exhorted me from such opposite points of view, that I really require a little rest and time to collect my thoughts in order to do what your Grace requires of me with a clear head, and after a full consideration of all the consequences.

The statement recently brought forward by so-called Catholic newspapers, to the effect that in the affair of the pastor of Mering I had given a judgment which had been required of me, is a pure invention. No one has desired such a judgment from me, and I have not even had the opportunity of uttering an opinion on this subject. Your Grace could easily have this confirmed by the proper authorities at the Government Offices. — I remain, respectfully, your Grace's most obedient servant,

J. V. DÖLLINGER.

MUNICH, *March* 14*th*, 1871.

IX.

ARCHBISHOP VON SCHERR TO DÖLLINGER.

(March 17th, 1871.)

REVEREND SIR,—Although I am willing, in consequence of your honoured letter of the 14th (received on the 16th) inst., to prolong the time that expired with the 15th inst. to the 31st inst., I must add the remark that after this date I shall not be in a position to grant any further prolongation.

Continuing in the meanwhile to implore God that He may guide your resolutions,—I remain, Reverend Sir, in constant high esteem, yours faithfully,

✠ GREGORIUS,
Archbishop of Munich-Freising.

MUNICH, *March 17th*, 1871.

X.

DÖLLINGER TO ARCHBISHOP VON SCHERR.

(March 28th, 1871.[1])

MY LORD ARCHBISHOP,—Your Grace has invited me in two letters to make a declaration of my position to the Romish Resolutions of the 18th July 1870 which have been proclaimed by you. From the circle of your Cathedral Chapter, the report has spread that you meditate proceeding against me with such pains and penalties as are usually employed only against priests who have incurred the guilt of grave, moral transgressions, and even then only in

---

[1] In a letter dated March 20th, 1871, Döllinger says: "We must mutually confirm and refresh one another, in order that we may be able to stoutly sustain the conflict we have not sought, but which has been pressed upon us, and in order that we may preserve the *depositum* of truth for coming generations. Were even we to show ourselves submissive, the world would have to believe that the love of truth had completely died out among the Catholic clergy, and that the priesthood was now nothing but a profession. The moral bankruptcy of the clergy is already, without that, a *fait accompli* in public opinion.— The contest will bring to light a number of new, *i.e.* of hitherto unnoticed and unknown facts, to which I shall contribute my mite. In the first place, my letter to the Archbishop will appear in print."

very rare cases. This is to take place if I do not, within an appointed time, declare my submission to the two new articles of faith, viz. the omnipotence and the infallibility of the pope.

At the same time, an assurance is given that another meeting and deliberation of German bishops will take place very soon at Fulda. On an Assembly of all German bishops being held at Würzburg in 1848, I had the honour of receiving an invitation to it, and took part in its discussions. Your Grace could perhaps secure to me at the approaching Assembly also, not indeed an opportunity of taking part in the deliberations, but only a gracious audience for a few hours.

Before that high Assembly I am prepared to prove the following propositions, which for the present situation of the German Church, and for my personal position, may be of decisive importance:—

First. The new articles of faith rest for their establishment from the Scriptures on the passages Matt. xvi. 18, John xxi. 17, and as far as the infallibility is concerned on the passage Luke xxii. 32, with which, biblically considered, it stands and falls. Now we are bound by a solemn oath, which I have taken twice, not to accept or expound the Scriptures "in any other way than according to the unanimous agreement of the Fathers." The Fathers of the Church have all without exception expounded the passages in question in a sense entirely different from the new Decree, and especially in the passage Luke xxii. 32 they were far from seeing an infallibility granted to all popes. Accordingly, if I were willing to accept the Decrees with this interpretation, without which they are deprived of all biblical foundation, I should forswear myself. As I have already stated, I am willing to demonstrate this before the assembled bishops.

Second. In several pastoral letters and manifestoes of recent date from the bishops, the opinion is maintained, or an historical proof is attempted, that the new doctrine of papal omnipotence over every individual Christian, and of papal infallibility in decisions of faith as proclaimed at Rome, has always been believed and taught universally, or, at all events, almost universally in the Church from the earliest times and throughout all the centuries. This assertion rests, as I am ready to prove, on a complete misunderstanding of ecclesiastical tradition in the first thousand years of the Church, and on a distortion of her history; it contradicts the clearest facts and evidences.

Third. I offer further to bring forward proofs that the bishops of the Romance countries, Spain, Italy, South America, and France, who formed the enormous majority at Rome, had, together with their clergy, as regards the papal power, already been led astray by books of doctrine out of which they had derived their knowledge during their college years, for the passages quoted in these books as proofs are for the most part false, fabricated, or garbled. This I will prove, first, from the two principal works and favourite text-books of the present theological schools and colleges, the Moral Theology of St. Alphonse Liguori, especially in the tract it contains on the pope, and from the Theology of Perrone the Jesuit; second, from the writings of Archbishop Cardoni and Bishop Ghilardi, which were distributed in Rome at the time of the Council; and finally, from the Theology of the theologian Schwetz of Vienna.

Fourth. I appeal to the fact, and offer to prove it in public, that two General Councils and several popes as early as the fifteenth century decided the question of the extent of the pope's power and infallibility by solemn decrees which were proclaimed by the Councils, and repeatedly confirmed by the popes, and that the Decrees of the 18th July 1870 stand in glaring contradiction to these Resolutions, whence it is impossible that they should be binding.

Fifth and last. I think I shall be able to prove that the new Decrees are simply irreconcilable with the Constitutions of the European States, especially with that of Bavaria; and that by the oath of fealty to the Constitution which I have but lately again renewed on my entrance into the Upper House, I find it impossible to accept the new Decrees, and as their necessary sequence the Bulls "Unam Sanctam," and "Cum ex apostolatus officio," the Syllabus of Pius IX., and so many other papal dicta and laws which are now to be regarded as infallible decisions, and which stand in indissoluble conflict with the laws of the State. On this point I appeal to the verdict of the Faculty of Law in Munich, and, at the same time, I offer to leave it to the decision of any German Faculty of Law your Grace may care to name.

For the conference that has been proposed or rather implored by me, I have only two conditions to lay down. The first is, that my statements, with any possible replies, may be recorded, and their publication afterwards permitted; the second is, that a man of scientific training of my own choice may be allowed to be present at the conference.

Should this be unattainable at Fulda and before the German bishops, I must humbly set forth another request. May your Grace be pleased to form a commission of members of your Cathedral Chapter, before which I might be able to bring forward my case in the manner just described. Several of these reverend gentlemen are doctors, and were at one time professors of theology, and formerly my own pupils. I may thus cherish the hope that it will be more agreeable for them to meet me in a calm discussion, and, if possible, to refute me with reasons and facts, than to compose from the judgment seat spiritual criminal sentences and then to lay them before your Grace "to fulminate" them, as the saying is. I should esteem it a great honour if your Grace would be willing to preside at the conference, and set me right in reference to any errors in my quotations and expositions of evidences and facts, which, I am sure, would only redound to the advantage of the truth. Further, if you intend to make use of your episcopal power over me, I may still, I think, hope that it is the best, the noblest, and the most beneficial attribute of that power, and the one most Christlike, I mean the teaching office, that you will prefer to exercise upon me first. Should I be convinced by evidences and facts, I herewith bind myself to make a public recantation, refuting and retracting all I have ever written on this subject. In any case, the results could only be such as would be desirable for the general peace of mind as well as for the Church. For it is here not simply a question of my own person. Thousands of the clergy, and hundreds of thousands of laymen, think as I do, and regard the new articles of faith as inadmissible. Up to the present not a single one, even of those who have sent in a declaration of submission, has said to me that he is really convinced of the truth of these propositions. All my friends and acquaintances confirm me by asserting that their experience is the same. "Nobody believes them," is what I hear from day to day out of every mouth. A conference such as I propose, together with the publication of the minutes, will therefore certainly afford a much clearer insight into the matter, and one such as countless numbers are longing for.

Your Grace will perhaps refer me to the pastoral letter that appeared recently in your name, as a source from which I can derive sufficient instruction and correction of my opinion. But I must confess that it has produced the very opposite effect upon me, and I will enter into an engagement to prove that it contains a long series of misunderstood, garbled, mutilated or invented evidences, which together with the suppression of important facts and opposing evidences, forms a picture that is altogether unlike actual tradition. He whom your Grace entrusted with this task has certainly not devised the forgeries himself, but has borrowed in good faith from others (Cardoni, etc.). Should he, however, be meditating a defence of his work in the proposed conference, he would find me ready within a few hours either to prove my assertion, or in case I should not succeed, to make a public apology to him. But there is one condition which, on account of the importance of the matter, I think I must make, namely, that the Government be requested to allow an official conversant with history and canon-law to be present at the conference as a witness. As the affair is also of great importance for all Governments, we may take it for granted that this will not be refused on the part of the State.

In the past history of the Church there is no lack of facts which show that my proposal is in full keeping with the principles as well as the practice of the Church. Thus in the year 411 A.D. a conference of 286 Catholic and 279 Donatist bishops was held in three sittings under the presidency of the imperial government-official Marcellinus, when the controversial doctrine of the Church was discussed. At the conclusion the president decided in favour of the Catholic bishops. In the year 1433 A.D., Bohemian Calixtines appeared at the Council of Basel; a Decree that had been issued eighteen years previously at the Synod of Constance on the Communion in one kind was now subjected to a renewed discussion and examination, which resulted in the "Compacts" that were acknowledged also by the Papal See, and which make a very important and far-reaching concession to the Bohemians—a concession derogatory to the earlier resolution. A still greater similarity to the negotiations proposed by me is to be found in the conference so celebrated in French history between Bishop Du Perron of Evreux and the Protestant statesman and scholar Du Plessis-Mornay, which took place at Fontainebleau, in the year 1600 A.D., at the request of King Henry IV. It was a question of proving that a considerable number of passages had been forged or incorrectly quoted by Mornay in his book on the Eucharist. Henry himself presided, and the most respected men of both Churches were present as witnesses. After a few days, when a number of passages cited by Mornay had been examined, the conference was broken off by the illness of the latter, but produced in the highly-wrought minds of the people of that time an effect that was uncommonly favourable to the Catholic cause.

Most Reverend, my Lord Archbishop, I leave it entirely to your judgment what form you give the conference desired by me, and which will certainly be welcome to countless Catholics in Germany, as also what other men you wish to invite or oppose to me. Your diocese has no lack of theologians by profession, who will certainly be quite ready to comply with your invitation. That a question of faith is just as much the affair of the laity as of the clergy, and that also the former are allowed to take part in the scientific investigation and establishment of tradition, is shown by the practice of the Church, and has been acknowledged by popes and theologians. Here, where it is a matter of historical proofs, I gladly subject myself to the judgment of the most eminent German historians and of the Catholic faith. Let men like Ficker, Reumont, Hoefler, Arneth, Kampschulte,

Cornelius, Lorenz, Wegele, Aschbach pass judgment, whether my reasoning is critically and historically correct or not.

On a former occasion your Grace honoured my book on the earliest, *i.e.* the Apostolic Age of the Church with your approval, and in Germany generally it was regarded on the Catholic side as a faithful picture of the times of the Church's foundation; even from Jesuit and Ultramontane circles no important censure has been expressed. But if the new Decrees contain the truth, then I shall be met with the reproach of having perverted the history of the apostles. The whole portion of my book on the constitution of the earliest Church, and my representation of the relation in which Paul and the rest of the apostles stood to Peter, are in that case thoroughly false, and I should have to condemn my own book, and confess that I have never understood either St. Luke's Acts of the Apostles or the Apostolic Epistles.

The new Vatican doctrine confers on the pope the attribute of *the whole fulness of power* (totam plenitudinem potestatis) over the whole Church as well as over every individual layman,—a power which is at the same time to be truly episcopal and again specifically papal, which is to include in itself all that affects faith, morals, duties of life, and discipline, and which can, without any mediation whatever, seize and punish, bid and forbid every one, the monarch as well as the labouring man. The wording is so carefully chosen that there remains for the bishops absolutely no other position and authority than that which belongs to papal commissaries or plenipotentiaries. As every student of history and of the Fathers will admit, the episcopate of the ancient Church is thus dissolved in its inmost being, and an apostolic institution, to which, according to the judgment of the Church Fathers, the greatest significance and authority in the Church belongs, fades into an unsubstantial shadow. No one can really conceive of two bishops existing in the same diocese, one who is also the pope, and one who is only a bishop; for a papal vicar or diocesan commissary is indeed not really a bishop nor a successor of the apostles. He may be in possession of great power in consequence of the authority conferred upon him by Rome, *i.e.* as long as he is permitted to govern by him from whom he receives his commission; just as great power also belongs to a Jesuit or mendicant friar who is furnished by the pope with a plenitude of privileges; and I am well aware that this prospect of an increase in their power has been offered to the bishops in Rome,—that it has often been said to them: The more irresistible the pope is, the more powerful will you be, for rich rays of glory will descend upon you from the fulness of his power. The bishops of the minority saw through the illusion of these promises. They have well recognised that, as the official "Analytical Synopsis" shows, if the universal episcopacy of the pope is established, they will, perhaps, still be dignitaries of the Church, but no longer real bishops. You yourself, most Reverend Sir, took part in the deputation which made the most urgent remonstrances to the pope on the 15th of July,—remonstrances which Herr von Ketteler tried to emphasise still more by a prostration. As is well known, these remonstrances have been vain. The entire consolation bestowed on the prelates who were lamenting the loss of their ancient ecclesiastical dignity was limited to the announcement in the Decree that the episcopal power was an "ordinary" one (viz. a "potestas ordinaria subdelegata," as the Roman Canonists are wont to express themselves), and that the pope regarded it as his duty to uphold them. This was supported by a mutilated dictum of Gregory the Great, a passage which, had it been cited in full with others, would certainly have shown the world that this pope of the seventh century rejected such a universal episcopate, as has now been established, with the profoundest horror as a blasphemous usurpation.

During the Council, as well as previous to it, there was no lack of petitions, remonstrances, and warnings. You yourself, most Reverend Sir, took part in them by your signature. In an Address delivered to the pope on the 12th January, and signed by you, the bishops of the minority declared that " the sayings and actions of the Church Fathers, the *genuine* documents of history, and even the Catholic conception of doctrine presented some serious difficulties which were opposed to the proclamation of the doctrine of infallibility." They were at that time, as they say, filled with alarm at a discussion of these difficulties, and begged the pope not to impose upon them the necessity of such a deliberation, *i.e.* to renounce the dogma of his infallibility. But when the pope insisted on the Council taking the matter in hand, the German bishops desired conferences at which the question of the infallibility should be entered into in detail, and which should be held by deputations chosen from both parties. These were not granted, and they were confined to speeches in the Aula, where, indeed, any regular discussion was impossible. But to show how indispensable and exceedingly urgent such testing conferences would have been, I will here cite but one example. In a memorial, which has now been printed, a considerable number of Italian bishops demanded that the papal infallibility should be raised to an article of faith, because it had been taught by two men, both of whom were Italians and the pride of their nation, viz. those two bright shining lights of the Church, Thomas Aquinas and Alphonse of

Liguori.[1] Now, it was well known, and had already been noticed by Gratry as well as by myself, that Aquinas had been deluded by a long series of invented evidences, as he, indeed, in proof of his doctrine, only appeals to such forgeries, and never to the genuine passages of the Fathers or Councils. And as far as Liguori is concerned, one glance at his writings is sufficient to show an experienced theologian that he handled forged passages in a much worse way than Aquinas. My reference to the fraud of which Thomas had been a victim, had caused a great sensation in Rome; the author of a paper that was at that time written in Rome, and directed against me, says that round about him it was received with cries of disapproval.[2] It would accordingly have been unavoidably necessary to subject the matter to examination. This examination, it is true, had it been comprehensive and thorough, would have led very far; it would have produced the result that the theory of papal infallibility had been introduced into the Church only by a long chain of purposeful fictions and forgeries, and had then been propagated and confirmed by violence, by suppression of the old doctrine, and by the manifold ways and means that

[1] *Vide:* The Official Collection of Documents on the Œcumenical Council, ii. 153.

[2] *De Romani Pontificis supremâ potestate docendi disputatio theologica*, Neapoli 1870, p. 50: "En tota clamorum, quos circumcirca audimus, causa."

are at the disposal of a sovereign. All endeavours, remonstrances, and petitions were thus in vain; nothing was granted, and that although they had before their eyes the so often cited example of the Council of Florence, where the assertion of the Greeks, to the effect that forged texts of the Fathers had been laid before them, led to examinations and discussions which lasted for months, and were conducted with the greatest care. It is certainly well known to your Grace that when a true Œcumenical Council was to issue Decrees, the most exact and mature examination of tradition was always required as a condition of their validity. What a contrast, too, in this respect were the proceedings at Trent, compared with what happened at Rome in 1870! It is true that the paper of Archbishop Cardoni, which had already been accepted in the preparatory Commission, and was now to pass for argument with the assembled bishops, would not have stood examination for a single hour.

In the whole history of the Church, among those Councils that have the reputation of being universal, I am only aware of one at which, as at the recent Council, the men in power prevented a thorough discussion of tradition, and that is the Second Council of Ephesus in 449 A.D. There, at the so-called Robber Synod, it took place with violence and tumultuous tyranny; at the Vatican Council, it was the order of business imposed on the Assembly, the papal Commission, and the will of the majority, that did not suffer a proper and thorough examination, which, it is true, would have brought some very troublesome and disagreeable things to light, but it would have also preserved the Church from a confusion which seems lamentable even in your eyes. But if, after all, you assert that the Vatican Assembly was perfectly "free," I suppose you use the word "free" in a sense which it otherwise does not convey in theological circles. A Council is only theologically "free" when there is a free examination and discussion of all scruples and difficulties, and when the objections are admitted and examined according to the rules required by the ascertainment of tradition. That to this end not even the most modest beginning has been made, and that, indeed, the immense majority of bishops from the Romance countries lacked either the will or the proper discernment for separating truth from falsehood, right from wrong, is proved by the writings which have appeared in Italy, and which have been distributed in Rome, as, for example, those of Ghilardi the Dominican and Bishop of Mondovi. This is also further proved by the fact that hundreds of these bishops could, without blushing, appeal to the inviolable authority of Alphonse Liguori.

When the Jesuits formed the plan of having the papal absolutism raised to an article of faith in Church and State, in doctrine and administration, they invented, as is well known, the so-called *sacrificio dell' intelletto*, and assured their adherents and disciples, nay actually convinced many, and among them even bishops, that the most beautiful homage due to God, and the noblest Christian heroism, consist in a man's renouncing his own mental judgment, his self-acquired knowledge and self-gained power of discernment, and in throwing himself in blind faith into the arms of the infallible papal " magisterium " as the only sure source of religious knowledge. In the eyes of countless numbers this Order has, it is true, to a great extent succeeded in raising mental sloth to the dignity of a religious meritorious sacrifice, and sometimes in moving even men, who by their general education would certainly have been well capable of instituting such an historical investigation, to a renunciation of it. But the German bishops, so far as one may judge from their pastoral letters, have not yet descended to this stage of infatuation. They still leave to human knowledge, to human scrutiny and investigation, their respective rights and spheres of operation. They appeal to history, as did also the pastoral letter that appeared in your name.

In the pastoral letter of Bishop Lothar von Kübel of Freiburg, we read on page 9 : " Does the pope receive new revelations? Can he make new articles of faith ? Certainly not. He can only declare that a doctrine is contained in the Holy Scriptures and tradition, accordingly is revealed by God, and therefore to be believed by all." I do not doubt that your Grace and the remaining German bishops fully agree with these words. But then in the present complicated position of the Church it is a purely historical question which must be treated and decided only with the means placed at our disposal for the purpose, and according to the rules which hold for every historical investigation, and for every ascertainment of facts of past ages, facts which accordingly belong to history. Pope and bishops must here of necessity put themselves, so to say, under the sovereignty of the Common Law, *i.e.* if their Resolutions are to have any stability they must employ those means of procedure, and undertake that examination of witnesses with the requisite sifting and critical searching, which, according to the unanimous agreement of all who, of all times and peoples, have been capable of judging in historical matters, is the only possible way of arriving at truth and certainty. Two questions ought then to have been and are still to be answered. First: Is it true that the three sayings of Christ in reference to Peter have been understood in the whole Church from the very beginning and through the centuries in the same sense as is now attached to them, namely, of an infallibility and boundless universal sovereignty which is thereby conferred on all popes? Second: Is it true that the Church tradition of all times, in the writings of the Fathers and the facts of history, shows the universal recognition of this papal double right?

If these questions must be answered in the negative, we may not, as Herr von Kübel and others do, appeal to the assistance of the Holy Ghost, which is assured to the pope, and to the obedience of faith which is therefore due to him; for whether he really is in enjoyment of this assistance is just what has to be historically proved. Where has this hitherto been done? Not at the Council; for there, as Cardoni's principal paper proves, they did not shun even forgeries, and gave a perfectly untruthful representation of tradition, with concealment of the most striking facts and contrary evidences. This it is that I now offer to prove.

And here I beg your Grace to consider that according to the nature of the thing, according to the express declaration of the pope, and according to the admission of all infallibilists, the doctrine we are now called upon to confess forms one, or rather the fundamental article of faith, and that it directly affects the question of the *regula fidei*, the rule of faith, which has to decide what is or what is not to be believed. In future every Catholic Christian when asked why he believes this or that, can and may give but the one answer: I believe or reject it because the infallible pope has bidden it to be believed or rejected. This highest principle of faith must never have been obscured in the Church, as it must of necessity have been stated as clear as daylight in the Scriptures; it must have ruled the whole Church like a brightly shining star, and that at all times and for all nations; it must have been put at the head of all instruction; and we are still all awaiting the explanation of how it is that until 1830 years had passed the Church did not hit upon the thought of formulating into an article of faith a doctrine which the pope, in the letter of the 28th October addressed to your Grace, calls "ipsum fundamentale principium catholicae fidei ac doctrinae!" How has it then been possible that for centuries the popes have winked at the denial of this fundamental article of faith by whole countries and in whole theological schools? And was there a unity of the Church where there was a difference in the very fundaments of belief? And—may I further add?—how is it then that your Grace yourself resisted so long and so persistently the proclamation of this dogma? You answer, "Because it was not opportune!" But can it ever be "inopportune" to give believers the key to the whole building of faith, to proclaim the fundamental article on which all others depend? Are we not now all standing before a dizzy abyss which opened itself before our eyes on the 18th July?

Whoever wishes to measure the immense range of the recent Resolutions, I strongly recommend him carefully to read the third and fourth chapters of the Decrees together, and then let him picture to himself what a system of the most complete universal dominion and spiritual dictatorship we have here to face. It is the whole fulness of power over the collective Church, as well as over every individual, claimed by the popes since Gregory VII., and expressed in the numerous bulls since "Unam Sanctam," which is henceforth to be believed by every Catholic, and acknowledged in public life. This power is boundless and incalculable; it can interfere everywhere, as Innocent III. says, where sin is, can punish everybody, brooks no appeal, and is absolute arbitrariness; for the pope, as Boniface VIII. expressed it, carries every privilege in the shrine of his breast. As he has become infallible, he can, at any moment, with the one little word "orbi" (thereby addressing the whole Church), make every statute, every doctrine, and every postulate, an infallible and irrevocable article of faith. As opposed to him, there exists no right, no personal or corporative freedom, or, as the Canonists say, "the tribunals of God and the pope are one and the same." This system bears the mark of its Romance origin on its brow, and will never be able to penetrate into Germanic countries. As Christian, as theologian, as historian, as citizen, I cannot accept this doctrine. I cannot do so as a Christian, because it is incompatible with the spirit of the gospel, and with the lucid sayings of Christ and the apostles; it simply wishes to establish the kingdom of this world, which Christ declined to do, and to possess the sovereignty over the congregations, which Peter refused for every one else, as well as for himself. I cannot do so as a theologian, because the whole genuine tradition of the Church stands irreconcilably opposed to it. I cannot do so as an historian, because, as such, I know that the persistent endeavours to realise this theory of a universal sovereignty has cost Europe streams of blood, distracted and ruined whole countries, shaken to its foundations the beautiful organic edifice of the constitution of the older Church, and begotten, nursed, and maintained the worst abuses in the Church. Finally, I must reject it as a citizen, because, with its claims on the submission of States and monarchs and the whole political order of things to the papal power, and by the exceptional position claimed by it for the clergy, it lays the foundation for an endless and fatal discord between the State and the Church, between the clergy and the laity. For I cannot conceal from myself the fact that this doctrine, the consequences of which were the ruin of the old

German Empire, in case it should become dominant in the Catholic part of the German nation, would at once plant the germ of an incurable disease in the recently restored empire.[1] — I remain, your most obedient servant,

J. V. DÖLLINGER.

[1] I have just read the following statements in the official organ of the Romish Curia and of the Jesuits, viz. in the *Civiltà*, for March 18th, 1871, p. 664 : —

"The pope is the chief justice of the Civil Law. In him the two powers, the spiritual and temporal, meet together as in their head ; for he is the vicar of Christ, who is not only Eternal Priest, but also King of kings and Lord of lords ; " and a little further on : " The pope, by virtue of his high dignity, is at the head of both powers."

XI.

ARCHBISHOP VON SCHERR'S PASTORAL LETTER.

(April 2nd, 1871.)

GREGORIUS, by the mercy of God and the grace of the Holy Apostolic See, Archbishop of Munich-Freising, Domestic Prelate and Assistant at the Throne of His Papal Holiness, etc. etc., to the whole body of venerable Clergy, and to all the Faithful of the Archbishopric, greeting and blessing in the Lord!

On the 29th March last, Dr. von Döllinger, Provost and Professor of Theology, addressed to Us a declaration of his position to the General Vatican Council and its Resolutions up to the present, which he, at the same time, put at the disposal of the Augsburg *Allgemeine Zeitung*,[1] where it has already been given to the public. This publication compels us publicly and emphatically to call the attention of the reverend clergy and the faithful of our diocese to the principal errors which are contained in this exceedingly deplorable document, and which will separate the author

[1] See No. 90, Extra Supplement, March 31st, 1871.

from the Catholic Church if he persists in maintaining them.

1. The author requires that he may be allowed, in an Assembly of bishops or theologians, to bring forward proofs that the Decrees of Faith of the fourth sitting of the Vatican Council are not contained either in the Holy Scriptures, as the Fathers understood them, or in tradition, according to its genuine history; but rather that the latter has been forged by means of fabricated or distorted documents, and that the Decrees themselves are opposed to former ecclesiastical decisions.

Now there is not here a question which has first to be decided, and, consequently, to be previously carefully examined. The matter is already decided. A General Council, legally summoned, freely assembled, and presided over by the Supreme Head of the Church, has, after careful examination, expounded, formulated, and defined the Catholic doctrine of the Primacy of the Roman Pope. Every Catholic Christian now knows what the Church sets forth to be believed. The Church to which Jesus Christ has promised His aid to the end of the world cannot require us to believe anything but what God has Himself revealed. Whoever, therefore, opposes the dictum of the Church opposes God. "Whoever neglects to hear the Church, let him be unto thee as an heathen and a publican" (Matt. xviii. 17).

2. The author asserts that "it is a purely historical question, which must be treated and decided only with the means placed at our disposal for the purpose, and according to the rules which hold for every historical investigation and for every ascertainment of facts of past ages—facts which accordingly belong to history." This, however, sets historical investigation above the Church. The decisions of the Church are given over to the ultimate and final judgment of historians, while the divinely ordained teaching office in the Church is done away with, and all Catholic truth questioned. Let science approach the Catholic doctrines of faith and test them by all means in the power of man; they will be able to stand every ordeal. The science of unbelief may set itself up against God and His revelation, against the Church and her Articles of Faith, but it will never be able to shake the rock on which the Lord has built His Church (Matt. xvi. 18).

3. The author declares that the Decrees of the 18th July last "are simply irreconcilable with the Constitutions of the European States, especially with that of Bavaria;" nay, further, "that this doctrine, the consequences of which were the ruin of the old German Empire, in case it should become dominant in the Catholic part of the German nation, would at once plant the germ of an incurable disease in the recently restored empire."

Against this entirely erroneous supposition and exceedingly malicious accusation, we do herewith, with all Our powers, protest most energetically, and declare it to be an unfounded defamation of the Catholic Church, her Supreme Head, her bishops and all her members, who will never cease to "render to Caesar that which is Caesar's, and to God that which is God's" (Matt. xxii. 21).

Most beloved Diocesans! The views, principles, and opinions that are brought forward in this document, and of which we have here only mentioned the chief, have been disseminated since the announcement of the Vatican Council with unchristian zeal and bitterness in many books, reviews, and daily papers. This is unfortunately the very document which will raise the long-cherished deplorable conjecture to the highest probability, that the author of this declaration has been the intellectual head of the whole movement set on foot against the Vatican Council, and which has begotten so much perplexity of mind and disquietude of conscience.

The equally numerous writings in refutation of these assertions have unfortunately not found a hearing in these circles of the Church's enemies.

But the matter has now assumed the form of a direct revolt against the Catholic Church by the public appearance of a man who has hitherto filled high appointments both in Church and State, and distinguished himself by his great services.

Most Beloved Diocesans! We are fully conscious of our official duty as bishop, and hence it is that we have not neglected to address these earnest words of warning to you, and also to take measures which had become an immediate necessity. In any further steps we shall have to take, we shall keep before our eyes no less the danger that threatens the Church in Germany than our love for our straying brother. We shall "not break the bruised reed nor quench the smoking flax" (Matt. xii. 20). But we shall also take care to protect our dear flock from error and seduction.

We appeal to the most reverend priests of our diocese in the words of St. Paul: "O Timothy, keep that which is committed to thy trust, avoiding profane and vain babblings, and oppositions of science falsely so called, which some professing have erred concerning the faith" (1 Tim. vi. 20, 21).

Most Beloved Diocesans! Pray all of you for the seriously imperilled salvation of the author of this heterodox declaration; pray for the Holy Church, especially in our dear German and Bavarian fatherland; pray for your deeply afflicted bishop, who now blesses you in the name of the Father, of the Son, and of the Holy Ghost. Amen.

This pastoral letter is to be communicated from the pulpit to the faithful according to requirement.

Given in Munich, Palm Sunday, 1871.

☩ GREGORIUS,
Archbishop of Munich-Freising.

XII.

THE ORDINARIATE OF MUNICH-FREISING TO DÖLLINGER.

(April 3rd, 1871.)

THE ORDINARIATE OF THE ARCHBISHOPRIC OF MUNICH-FREISING.

WE are commissioned by His Grace our Most Reverend Archbishop to send your Reverence the pastoral letter issued to-day, and contained in the accompanying number (14) of our Pastoral Gazette.

At the same time we have to make the further communication, that our Most Reverend Lord Archbishop has also this day prohibited all the candidates of theology in the diocese of Munich-Freising from further attendance at your lectures.

Further, it is our duty to remark that though His Grace is not able to prevent you from continuing your lectures, you can only do so in open opposition to your bishop, the lawful guardian of all instruction in the Catholic religion given in the diocese.

Finally, in consequence of your public declaration of the 29th ult., the Most Reverend Lord Archbishop requests you to reflect that the "Constitutio prima de ecclesiâ Christi," issued at the fourth sitting of the Vatican Council, is of a *dogmatic* nature, that opposition to the dogmas therein defined falls under the head of heresy, that formal heresy is followed *ipso facto* by the greater excommunication, which is reserved to the pope, and that therefore you will have to prove your conscience, and see whether you have not already fallen under this ecclesiastical censure.

Should your Reverence, which, God forbid! persist in maintaining the position taken up by the public declaration indicated, the public and solemn proclamation of your sentence would be inevitable, namely, that you have incurred exclusion from the Catholic Church to which you formerly rendered such valuable services.

Dr. Joseph von Prand,
Cathedral Provost and General Vicar.
K. Osterauer, *Secretary.*

Munich, *April 3rd*, 1871.

XIII.

THE ORDINARIATE OF MUNICH-FREISING TO DÖLLINGER.

(April 17th, 1871.)

THE ORDINARIATE OF THE ARCHBISHOPRIC OF MUNICH-FREISING.

By His Grace our Most Reverend Archbishop Gregorius of Munich-Freising, we have been this day commissioned to declare to your Reverence, as we now do, in the name of the same superior, that you have incurred the greater excommunication, with all the canonical consequences attached thereto.

Your Reverence has been made sufficiently acquainted with the Resolutions that were passed by the General Vatican Council on the 18th July last, confirmed by Pope Pius IX., and then solemnly proclaimed.

The position taken by your Reverence before the public, in opposition to the above-named Council, compelled his Lordship to demand from you a definite declaration in this matter, and to exhort you to a due submission.

This was done with words of paternal love on the 5th October last year, and on the 4th January this year.

Your Reverence delayed for a very long time sending a decided answer. However, your procrastinating letters of the 29th January and the 14th March of this year were received by his Lordship with the most patient indulgence.

At last your declaration of the 29th ult. appeared, which you at the same time gave into the hands of the public, and in which you not only refused to acknowledge the Resolutions of the Council, but also set up and defended an altogether heretical principle of faith, and hurled the most malicious charges against the Church.

In the Resolution sent to your Reverence on the 3rd inst., your attention was called in a clear and emphatic manner to the inevitable consequences of this step.

Nevertheless, up to the present, it has been followed by no intimation whatever that your Reverence does not intend to persevere in your opposition to the dicta of the Church.

Since, in this way, your Reverence has opposed, and is still constantly opposing, a conscious and obstinate denial to the clear and sure decrees of faith of the Catholic Church; since, further, you have not listened to the repeated fatherly exhortations and warnings of your Archbishop, but have rather brought your opposition to the Church before the public and enlisted followers; since, finally, the great danger thereby called into existence has outweighed the long and patient consideration for your high position in Church and State, as well as for your indubitable services as a teacher, in science and in public life,—in consequence of all this, I say, for the salvation of your own soul, and as a warning to others, the *excommunicatio major*, fixed by the ecclesiastical law for the *crimen haereseos externae et formalis*, and lately enacted by the General Vatican Council relative to its Decrees of the 18th July last, it has been necessary to pronounce the excommunication which you have *ipso facto* drawn down upon yourself through the above-mentioned offence against the Church, by a special judicial sentence which will be made public, and of which I herewith give you notice.

Dr. JOSEPH VON PRAND,
Cathedral Provost and General Vicar.

Munich, *April* 17th, 1871.

XIV.

THE ORDINARIATE OF MUNICH-FREISING TO THE PAROCHIAL OFFICE OF ST. LUDWIGS CHURCH IN MUNICH.

(April 18th, 1871.)

The Ordinariate of the Archbishopric of Munich-Freising herewith charges the Parochial Office of St. Ludwig's Church in this city to cause to be announced from the pulpit at divine service on Sunday next the 23rd inst., that "His Grace the Archbishop has issued a pastoral declaration to the Provost and Professor Dr. von Döllinger, as well as to the Court Beneficiary and Professor Dr. John Friedrich, to the effect that on account of their conscious, obstinate, and public denial of clear and certain ecclesiastical doctrines of faith, they have incurred the greater excommunication, with all the canonical consequences attached thereto."

A report is expected that this order has been carried out.

Dr. JOSEPH VON PRAND,
Provost of the Cathedral and General Vicar.

K. OSTERAUER, *Secretary.*

MUNICH, *April* 18*th*, 1871.

XV.

DÖLLINGER TO PASTOR WIDMANN OF TODTNAU.

(October 18th, 1874.[1])

REVEREND SIR,—Willingly do I proceed to answer the questions put to me, although as an old man, and as having very many claims on my attention, it will be of necessity in a brief form only.

1. As for myself, I consider that I belong by conviction to the Old Catholic Community. I believe it has a high mission to fulfil, and that in a threefold way:

(*a*) To bear testimony to the truth as held by the Early Church, and against the erroneous doctrines of papal universal supremacy and infallibility; and especially to be also a speaking and permanent protest against the baleful arbitrariness first practised by the present pope on the introduction of the Articles of Faith.

(*b*) A second vocation of the Old Catholic Com-

---

[1] Published as early as 1875, at first without the name of the addressee, in various daily papers, and among others in the *Deutscher Merkur*, No. 29.

munity is, in my eyes, to become by degrees and by gradual progress a Church which shall be free from delusion and superstition, and more conformable to the ancient one, before it was broken up by schism.

(*c*) Closely connected therewith is its third vocation, namely, to serve as an instrument and a link of mediation for a future greater reunion of the disunited Christians and Churches. A beginning, though small, was made in this direction a few weeks ago at Bonn. I have great confidence in the progress of this work of peace.

2. I have no hope whatever that under the next, or one of the next popes, any important or essential change will be made for the better; and as far as I can see, all who know the condition of the Roman Curia and the Roman clergy are just as hopeless as I in this respect. In the whole of this papal community within and without the confines of Italy, there is no longer any moving power but one, in the presence of which all others, the episcopacy, the cardinalate, the spiritual orders, the schools, etc., remain passive—and that is the Order of the Jesuits. It is the soul and sovereign of the whole of the Roman Church. This will probably remain so also under a new pope, for this Order is indispensable, and cannot even exist without ruling or wishing to rule.

Formerly, before 1773, there existed various counterpoises in the Church. The other Orders were then still strong and full of vitality; now they are either powerless shadows or half-willing, half-unwilling satellites of the dominating Jesuit constellation; and the Roman Curia, in order to remain a curia, to preserve its ecclesiastical monopoly, its financial resources, etc., is compelled to rely on the Jesuits, *i.e.* to be subservient to them and their impulses. And the Jesuits are the incarnation of superstition united with despotism. To rule mankind by means of the pope, who has become subservient to them—this is their task, their aim, and their art, which they practise in a masterly way. Hence their endeavours to make religion mechanical, the *sacrificio dell' intelletto*, which they highly recommend, the training of souls to unconditioned and blind obedience, etc. But what the condition of the Roman community is now, since the 18th July 1870, and what is to be expected for the immediate future, you may conclude from the fact that it has been possible to bring about the greatest monstrosity that has ever occurred in the domain of theological doctrine without a single voice being raised in opposition to it, I mean the solemn proclamation of Alphonse Liguori as *Doctor ecclesiae*, consequently classing him with Augustine, Ambrose, etc.,—a man whose false morals, perverse worship of the Virgin, constant use of the grossest fables and forgeries, make his writings a storehouse of errors and lies. In the whole range of Church history I do not know a single example of such a terrible and such a pernicious confusion.

And yet every one is silent on this point, and in all theological colleges the growing generation of the clergy is being poisoned with these books of Liguori.

Such a state of things cannot, of course, last long; sooner or later a reaction for the better must set in, somewhere and somehow; but it is just this How and this Where which are hidden from our eyes.

To your third question, what I advise you to do, I answer: Follow your own convictions, and do not allow yourself to be deluded by the pretexts of unity which ought to be preserved, and of unconditioned obedience, whereby every erroneous idea and every deformity of religion, however terrible, is palliated. What we can and ought to do in this wretched condition is to bear testimony before God and the world, and to give the truth as recognised by us the honour which is due to it. It is the general indifference, and the indolent attitude of the clergy, which has only their own comfort in view, that have brought down this evil of the Vatican upon our heads. The greater the number of those who confess the truth and free themselves from false doctrine and implicit obedience, the greater becomes the hope of recovery.—In haste, yours most respectfully,

J. V. DÖLLINGER.

XVI.

DÖLLINGER TO AN OLD CATHOLIC AT DORTMUND.

(June 23rd, 1878.[1])

DEAR SIR,—The statements in the paper you sent me are malicious lies as regards both Prof. Friedrich and myself. This is now the fourteenth time that my submission has been announced by Ultramontane papers, and it will often occur again. Rest assured that I shall not dishonour my old age with a lie before God and man.—With kind regards, I remain, yours devotedly,

J. V. DÖLLINGER.

[1] *Deutscher Merkur*, 1878, p. 221.

XVII.

DÖLLINGER TO PROFESSOR MICHELIS.

(May 1st, 1879.[1])

. . That nothing of any importance in the sense of an improvement of the ecclesiastical situation is to be expected from Leo XIII., was to my mind quite certain from the time when he declared to the cardinals, who were one and all creatures of his predecessor, that he would not undertake anything without consulting them and without their sanction. That he gave the cardinal's hat to a Newman, who stands so high above the Roman *vulgus praelaticum* in intellect and knowledge, can only be explained by the fact that the real views of the man are not known in Rome. Had Newman written in French, Italian, or Latin, several of his books would now be standing in the Index.

For a number of years I have now been investigating the influences of the Papacy through all the centuries, and have studied especially the history of single States and established Churches, according to

[1] *Deutscher Merkur*, 1879, p. 158.

the forms they have assumed through the working of Rome. The conclusion is: Rome's influence is much more harmful and ruinous than I had even any idea of, say, before 1860. In Germany, if we investigate the causes of the decay of our old empire, this is self-evident. In the Romance countries it is still worse. . . .

XVIII.

DÖLLINGER TO DR. ROBERT J. NEVIN, RECTOR OF THE ANGLO-AMERICAN CHURCH IN ROME.[1]

(May 4th, 1879.)

MY DEAR NEVIN, — I suppose your influence is sufficiently strong to get a short article or notice inserted in one of the Liberal papers (*contradicting*)[2] the lies that have been spread over all Europe respecting my contemplated or consummated submission to the Vatican decrees.

I have neither written nor done anything which could have given occasion to such a rumour. The circumstances which are mentioned in some papers are gratuitous inventions.

I have only three weeks ago published a lecture (*Allgem. Zeitung*, 6, 7, 8 April),[3] in which I state in

---

[1] A copy of this letter, which Döllinger wrote in English, was kindly placed at the editor's disposal by Dr. Nevin.

[2] This or some such word was omitted in the original by an oversight.

[3] "Garcin de Tassy and India," now printed in the *Akademische Vorträge*, vol. ii. See p. 297.

so many words, that nobody possessing a scientific culture of mind can ever accept the decrees of the Vatican Council.

Having devoted during the last nine years my time principally to the renewed study of all the questions connected with the history of the Popes and the Councils, and, I may say, gone again over the whole ground of ecclesiastical history, the result is, that the proofs of the falsehood of the Vatican decrees amount to demonstration. When I am told that I must swear to the truth of those doctrines, my feeling is just as if I were asked to swear that two and two make five and not four.

Pray, my dear Nevin, let me have some more news of what is going on in Rome.

Perhaps you can also obtain the reception of a similar notice in one of the American papers.

Totus tuus,

J. DOELLINGER.

MUNICH, 4 *Mai*, 1879.

XIX.

A LADY OF HIGH RANK TO DÖLLINGER.

February 15th and 28th, 1880.)

B., *February* 15*th*, 1880.

REVEREND DOCTOR,—For years I have been imploring God from the depths of my heart that He will send down a beam of His divine love into your heart, in order that by this heavenly light you may recognise the abyss on the edge of which you are standing, and that you may thus be preserved from destruction. As the thought of your Reverence deprives me of my peace of mind, I have now resolved, however presumptuous this may seem to you, to entreat your own co-operation with this divine grace. Your Reverence's acute intellect has penetrated too far into the teachings of our holy religion not to know that when a priest so highly-favoured, talented, and enlightened as you are, sets himself up against the authority of the Church, and dies in disobedience to it, he has a much more terrible punishment to expect in eternity than others who had less knowledge, less grace, and hence less responsibility. A positive horror and an altogether indescribable feeling of pity seize hold upon me when I think of the awful future you are inevitably going to meet, if you do not now, in the eleventh hour, turn back. Oh, your Reverence, how I should like to beg you on my knees to have mercy on your unhappy soul, and save it from this most terrible of all fates! You know it and believe it? What, then, can prevent you from turning back? Is it regard for what individual persons will say? Or is it pride that will not admit an error? Oh, what is all this? How can one waver and hesitate when in the one scale, alongside a small span of time and a small piece of the apparent gold of human honour, lies an eternity full of the most indescribable woe; but in the other, as a recompense for an heroic resolution, everlasting and unending blessedness, the contemplation and possession of God!

The few who perhaps would dare to blame your step, cannot hereafter before God take your guilt upon themselves and bear your punishment for you; whereas the many Catholics, and still more the angels and saints in heaven who will greet your return with acclamations of the most blessed joy, will admire your humility and heroic conquest of self; all these will accompany your soul with their prayers, and stand by you in that hour from which none can escape. With touching eloquence your Reverence once depicted the death of St. Francis, closing with the words: "God grant us all such an end!" This saint will stand by you in that trying hour; he will strengthen and comfort you, if you now have the courage to become a humble son of the Church once more.

Oh, your Reverence, open your heart to the divine grace while there is still time! Delay not until it is too late! Invoke the blessed St. Francis!

With the warmest and sincerest wishes for your Reverence's welfare,

I subscribe myself,

※ ※ ※ ※

B., *February 28th*, 1880.

REVEREND SIR,—I cannot let this day[1] pass without repeating to your Reverence how very fervently I, yea, all good Catholics, are imploring God for you, that He will overwhelm you with an overflowing and irresistible ray of light and grace, and that you, being overpowered by it and constrained by the divine love, may fall at the Saviour's feet—nay, sink into His ever open arms, on to His divine heart—and there find the rest, the peace, and the salvation which you will never, nay, not in all eternity, enjoy elsewhere! Oh, your Reverence, what are ninety, what are a hundred years compared to eternity! What are all the honours of men, when it is a question of renouncing

---

[1] [Döllinger's birthday.—TRANSLATOR.]

these honours in order to escape the justice of God, and, what is more, His punishments! Of what avail is the past, with which one must break, if we can exchange for it the contemplation of God that maketh blessed! Do not let yourself by these human considerations be held back from doing that by which you will gain the joyful admiration of the whole Catholic world, and purchase yourself everlasting bliss and untold rewards in the other world. Oh, bethink yourself while there is still time! See how lovingly the Saviour waits for you, how, unmoved by the delay of your return, He adds one year after another to your life, and in His grace knocks again and again at the door of your heart! Do not keep Him waiting any longer! Answer at last His great love with your love for Him, with a true penitent return, and thus save yourself from everlasting death!

That your Reverence may find light and strength for this return in sincerest contrition, and after so long a life on earth may also secure the possession of God for all eternity, this is my sincerest wish to-day; this, too, is my prayer for you to the Mother of grace and to the seraphic saint whom your Reverence once so highly honoured, whose praise you so eloquently proclaimed. With this wish and prayer I remain, your Reverence's devoted

* * *

XX.

DÖLLINGER'S ANSWER TO THE LETTERS OF A LADY OF HIGH RANK.

(1880.)

. . . ABOVE all, I must offer you my sincere and deeply-felt thanks for your anxiety about my soul's salvation, which you have manifested in so courteous a manner in the letter you have addressed to me.

As to the subject-matter itself, had I to deal with a man, I should simply refer him to those facts and reasons which I published in the year 1871, when submission to the Vatican Decrees was demanded of me—facts and reasons, every one of which is, according to my conviction, that to-day is firmer than ever, unrefuted and irrefutable. But your Ladyship has probably never seen that document, or if it did come into your hands, you did not deem it worthy of notice. Presumably you have been told that everything I have asserted is untrue, and you have willingly composed yourself with this assertion, a thing which I regard as quite natural. Nevertheless, I am going to take the liberty of directing your attention to a few circumstances which perhaps may help to moderate your opinion about my position and conduct.

I am now in my eighty-first year, and was a public teacher of theology for forty-seven years, during which long period no censure, nor even a challenge that I should defend myself or make a better explanation, has ever reached me from ecclesiastical dignitaries either at home or abroad. I had *never* taught the new Articles of Faith advanced by Pius IX. and his Council. In my youth, when I studied at Bamberg and Würzburg, they were regarded as theological opinions, and many added "ill-founded" opinions. In me, who for almost half a century had to occupy myself daily with this subject and the questions affecting it, the conviction became stronger and stronger that these doctrines and claims are not only biblically, traditionally, and historically unfounded and erroneous, but also that even before they were raised to the rank and binding power of Articles of Faith, they had had the most detrimental effects on the Church, the State, and society. Then came the fatal year 1870. If I had obeyed the summons to affirm the new dogmas on oath, I should thereby have declared myself to have been an heretical teacher, and not only myself, but also my deceased teachers, as also a number of friends and colleagues who found themselves in the same position. It was in vain that I begged they would let me remain by the faith and confession to which I had hitherto been faithful without blame and without contradiction. Yesterday still orthodox, I was to-day a heretic worthy of excommunication, not because I had changed my teaching, but because others had considered it advisable to undertake the alteration, and to make opinions into Articles of Faith.

I ought, as the favourite expression of the Jesuits runs, "to make a sacrifice of my intellect" (*sacrificio dell' intelletto*). This is what your Ladyship also demands of me. But if I did so, in a question which is for the historical eye perfectly clear and unambiguous, there would then no longer be for me any such thing as historical truth and certainty; I should then have to suppose that my whole life long I had been in a world of dizzy illusion, and that in historical matters I am altogether incapable of distinguishing truth from fable and falsehood. The very ground would be thus taken away from under my feet, and that, too, for my religious views; since even our religion is founded, of course, on historical facts. I must first be convinced that the principal events narrated in the Gospels and the Acts of the Apostles are essentially true and inviolable, and this conviction must, for me, in accordance with my career and profession as teacher, be one which has been ascertained scientifically, *i.e.* acquired by my own mental endeavours, and guaranteed to me by careful investigation; for all that is asserted by the Church and her authority takes these historical facts for granted.

What would your Ladyship say if you were bidden, in the name of the pope, to believe and confess that the existence and the whole history of the first Napoleon was a myth and a fiction? Well, with the same inward certainty with which you are convinced of the existence of Napoleon and of the principal facts of his life, a certainty that no authority in the world can shake, I know that the Vatican Decrees are untrue. That is, I know, and not second or third hand, but by a careful life-long study of all the sources, that the two assertions of the absolute omnipotence and infallibility of the pope having always been believed and practised are false. It was only by a long concatenation of subtlety and violence, bribery, deceit, and fiction, that they succeeded step by step in repressing the old doctrine in spite of its thousand-fold proofs, and in procuring the final victory for the new one, which was devised in the interests of the monks. It is true that this required several centuries.

Your Ladyship is, as I have been assured, a lady of excellent mental culture, and accordingly acquainted with the classical French literature, with men like Bossuet and Fénelon, and is also aware that these men, and with them all bishops and theologians, in fact the whole of the French clergy before the Revolution, believed and taught the Gallican doctrine, that is, they rejected these very two Articles of Faith of the Vatican Council. Nevertheless, they were constantly confirmed in their offices by the popes, whereby the latter continually bore testimony to their perfect orthodoxy. If my bishop were to declare that he would release me from the ban on the condition that I would believe and confess what Bossuet and Fénelon, and hundreds of the most pious and most learned bishops with them, have taught about the pope, who would be more willing than I? Instead of this, an oath on the Vatican Resolutions is required of me, which would accordingly be for me open perjury, and that a double one; for, first, I should have to break the oath which was laid upon me on my entrance upon my official duties—the oath, namely, always to expound the Holy Scriptures in agreement with the interpretation of the holy Fathers; and, second, in the required oath I should have to carry out a moral self-destruction on myself. For with this oath I should testify that I had been teaching erroneous doctrines all my life, and that I had falsely understood and misinterpreted the history of the Church, the Fathers, and the Bible. And what should I gain thereby? First, I should not have another peaceful hour for the rest of my life, and then I should pass into the other world as a liar, laden with the fearful burden of perjury. . . .

XXI.

BISHOP HEFELE TO DÖLLINGER.

(June 10th, 1886.)

MOST REVEREND PROVOST,—Such an advanced age united to robust health, and such a freshness of mind as you enjoy, Most Reverend Provost, is the lot of but few. Although ten years younger, I already feel the infirmities of old age, and have therefore taken steps for the appointment of a coadjutor. But before I close my life's work I should like to take the liberty of once more addressing a few words to your Reverence and Grace, words which are prompted as much by the undying respect for the great scholar as by the grateful remembrance of all the good-will you have shown me formerly. These few words take the form of a hearty request. Forget, dear Sir, all the unfairness you have experienced at the hands of your temporary adversaries; generously forget all this, and to the joy of angels and men, make your peace with the Church, which you have so long and so gloriously defended. Do not cast aside my request abruptly as unauthorised, for it comes from a sincere and thankful

heart, and I know, nay, you yourself are aware of it, that tens of thousands join with me most sincerely in this request. Do you by this peace crown the glorious career of your life that has been so richly blessed.—
Yours most respectfully and devotedly,

Dr. Hefele, *B.* of *R*.

XXII.

ARCHBISHOP ANTONIUS VON STEICHELE TO DÖLLINGER.

(1878, 1879, and 1886.)

MUNICH, *Dec.* 12*th*, 1878.

MOST REVEREND AND RESPECTED PROVOST,—Of the letter of exhortation which I issued to the clergy and people of the Archbishopric of Munich-Freising on entering upon my episcopal office, I have very recently had a new edition published, intended as a souvenir for distribution among friends. I feel myself impelled to put this gift into your hands also as a souvenir, Most Reverend Provost, the teacher of my youth, towards whom I have always preserved my earlier admiration and sense of gratefulness. I trust you will accept these first words of mine to my diocesans in a charitable spirit, and at the same time permit me with the sincere assurance of my continued sympathy and friendly feeling to remain, Reverend Sir, yours devotedly,

✠ ANTONIUS,
Archbishop of Munich-Freising.

MUNICH, *Feb. 27th*, 1879.

MOST REVEREND AND RESPECTED PROVOST,—To-morrow you will celebrate your eightieth birthday. I hail this day with heartfelt sympathy. It is with the thankfulness of a pupil to the hoary-headed teacher, with the respect of a disciple for the honoured bearer of the richest knowledge, and with the love of an anxious bishop for the brother who unfortunately is not yet at one with him in that which is highest and most important, that I shall be hovering about you in the spirit to-morrow. These are the feelings, respected Provost, with which I pray the richest blessings of Heaven may rest on your festival day to-morrow, and be yours in the future days of your life, of which I trust God's goodness will still grant you a goodly number. And—you feel it before I mention it—for what gift of God could I pray more sincerely and heartily for you than for the grace that His lamp and His staff may lead you back to unity with that Church whose head, equally troubled on your behalf as is your bishop, would so gladly stretch out the hand of peace to you. May God in His goodness grant that this moment may arrive before the day draws nearer to its close and the night cometh,—to the joy of thousands, who, like myself, are yearning for it, and to the consolation of the Holy Church, separated from unity with which, the isolated soul can surely never find rest and peace.

In all that love and care of which the evening of the 21st January was so recently our witness,—I am, and remain, Most Respected Provost, yours most devotedly, ✠ ANTONIUS,
Archbishop of Munich and Freising.

MUNICH, *July* 30*th*, 1886.

MOST REVEREND AND RESPECTED PROVOST,— There are but few days which pass without my thinking of you with the old love and sympathy, and without my soul being moved with anxiety and prayer for your welfare and salvation. To-day, the eve of the festival of your name-day,[1] which you will keep to-morrow, offers me an opportunity of bearing testimony to my feelings. I too shall celebrate this festival with you, though I am sorry I cannot do so with unalloyed joy. It is tarnished by the thought that I cannot reach you the hand of brotherly love to mutual endeavours for Christ and His kingdom, that the respected teacher stands here and the grateful pupil there, that of all who are entrusted to his care the bishop must see just that one afar off whom with the love and warmth of his heart he would like to see nearest. It is this feeling which admonishes and urges your bishop to address

[1] [The day of St. Ignatius, the festival of the anniversary of Döllinger's Christian name.—TRANSLATOR.]

a few friendly and well-intentioned words to his dear brother, inviting and begging him to be reconciled to the Holy Catholic Church for which he was once so ardent, and for which he has worked by spoken and written words and actions that have been so richly blessed; he also begs him further to re-enter that communion in which he once felt such happiness.

Within the last few weeks, respected Provost, you have made such friendly advances and shown such good-will towards me on occasions of our meeting, that I make this appeal to you with courage and confidence. God has added an almost unusual number of days to the term of your life, and wonderfully blessed you with strength of body and mind. But who knows how long the days of grace for returning into the bosom of the Church will still be granted to you? I too am getting well-advanced in life, but may that happy day be reserved to my term of office as bishop on which I might lead you again into the Church of God and to her Chief Shepherd! It would be a cause of rejoicing for millions of believers, joy for the choirs of the blessed, and a pledge of your own eternal salvation.

Praying God in His mercy to grant that I may see this happy day,—I remain, yours most faithfully and devotedly, ✠ ANTONIUS,
Archbishop of Munich and Freising.

XXIII.

DÖLLINGER TO ARCHBISHOP VON STEICHELE.

(March 1st, 1887.)

MY LORD BISHOP,—I have long delayed—too long, you will say—fulfilling my promise given in my previous communication.[1]

For several weeks I have cherished the thought of representing to your Grace in a detailed account the most important reasons for my persistence in my present position. For this purpose I had also made some notes on paper. By degrees, however, I recognised that the material, on account of its importance and abundance, would grow into a pamphlet or book, and that I ought not to take up your Grace's precious time with such reading as this. Accordingly I content myself with mentioning a few facts simply in order to give your Grace an account of my present position and the condition of my mind.

First. In the anathema which the Cathedral

---

[1] This communication, undoubtedly a short announcement of the answer here printed, has not been found.

decision in Gratian, Causa 23 quaest. 5, c. 47, Excommunicatorum, explained it with logical accuracy as follows: "If any one shall out of true zeal have put a man to death who has been excommunicated, *nullam meretur poenitentiam.*"

Such things have been perpetrated on me by persons who directed the steps of Herr von Scherr, who was completely dependent on others, and these persons had been my own pupils formerly.

What crime had I committed that I should be subjected to the heaviest of all punishments, to a punishment which, according to the dicta of the Church, is heavier than sentence of death?

I had refused to recognise a Council which, except numbers, lacked all the conditions of validity fixed by theology; a Council at which there was notoriously no freedom, no thorough examination, and no statement of actual tradition; a Council whose very unexampled order of business proclaimed the servitude of the bishops. A very few days after his return, Archbishop von Scherr candidly communicated several facts to me which left me no doubt on this point, and to these were added other verbal and written opinions, all of which were to the same effect.

that the discipline of the same Mother Church may not be forsaken, impose on them in the above-mentioned way an act of penance by which they may be able to appease the eyes of the divine purity when directed against them, if in the aforesaid crime they should have by chance incurred any impurity according to human infirmities."

In the recently published work by Herr von Schulte, *Der Altkatholicismus*, we have an ample collection of such letters and testimonies from bishops. What then can be still said in extenuation in face of this host of most weighty voices? Your Grace is certainly far from being willing to designate these venerable colleagues, some of whom are still living, as liars and calumniators of the Church. Verily, in view of these reports and testimonies, one would like to veil one's head in pain and mourning for this disgrace of the Occidental Church—a disgrace that can never more be wiped out. The course of the Vatican Council is worse than that of the Synod at Ephesus in 449 A.D. For cunning and deceit, mental compulsion, business-like oppression under the appearance of free deliberation are worse things than physical ill-treatment and wild clamour, such as there was at Ephesus.

And now as to the doctrine itself, the new Articles of Faith which have been fabricated eighteen centuries after the time of the apostles, and are now to be forced upon the world as primeval truths, tenets of faith, by which the solemn decisions of three Œcumenical Councils are annulled (680, 1415, 1431 A.D.), in spite of their having been confirmed by the popes! And these new Articles of Faith are now and must be the foundation and corner-stones on which henceforth the firmness and inviolability of

decision in Gratian, Causa 23 quaest. 5, c. 47, Excommunicatorum, explained it with logical accuracy as follows: "If any one shall out of true zeal have put a man to death who has been excommunicated, *nullam meretur poenitentiam.*"

Such things have been perpetrated on me by persons who directed the steps of Herr von Scherr, who was completely dependent on others, and these persons had been my own pupils formerly.

What crime had I committed that I should be subjected to the heaviest of all punishments, to a punishment which, according to the dicta of the Church, is heavier than sentence of death?

I had refused to recognise a Council which, except numbers, lacked all the conditions of validity fixed by theology; a Council at which there was notoriously no freedom, no thorough examination, and no statement of actual tradition; a Council whose very unexampled order of business proclaimed the servitude of the bishops. A very few days after his return, Archbishop von Scherr candidly communicated several facts to me which left me no doubt on this point, and to these were added other verbal and written opinions, all of which were to the same effect.

that the discipline of the same Mother Church may not be forsaken, impose on them in the above-mentioned way an act of penance by which they may be able to appease the eyes of the divine purity when directed against them, if in the aforesaid crime they should have by chance incurred any impurity according to human infirmities."

In the recently published work by Herr von Schulte, *Der Altkatholicismus*, we have an ample collection of such letters and testimonies from bishops. What then can be still said in extenuation in face of this host of most weighty voices? Your Grace is certainly far from being willing to designate these venerable colleagues, some of whom are still living, as liars and calumniators of the Church. Verily, in view of these reports and testimonies, one would like to veil one's head in pain and mourning for this disgrace of the Occidental Church—a disgrace that can never more be wiped out. The course of the Vatican Council is worse than that of the Synod at Ephesus in 449 A.D. For cunning and deceit, mental compulsion, business-like oppression under the appearance of free deliberation are worse things than physical ill-treatment and wild clamour, such as there was at Ephesus.

And now as to the doctrine itself, the new Articles of Faith which have been fabricated eighteen centuries after the time of the apostles, and are now to be forced upon the world as primeval truths, tenets of faith, by which the solemn decisions of three Œcumenical Councils are annulled (680, 1415, 1431 A.D.), in spite of their having been confirmed by the popes! And these new Articles of Faith are now and must be the foundation and corner-stones on which henceforth the firmness and inviolability of the whole Catholic doctrinal edifice is to rest. The old principle, "Nihil innovetur, nisi quod traditum est," so often insisted upon by all the Fathers, has now been turned into the opposite. In order to be consistent, all the older text-books of theology ought now to be re-written or prohibited; for they all rest upon tradition, which would only be a phantom if it did not hold fast to the tenet that every innovation which is contrary to the old doctrine is false, and to be rejected.

I confess that there was a time—in the years succeeding 1836—when I myself sincerely wished to be able to accept and demonstrate the so-called papal system. At that period, I saw that the Order of Jesuits was endeavouring, with the whole of its rapidly growing power, to bring this doctrine to an exclusive acceptation, and that for this purpose it was supported and encouraged by Rome and a great part of the episcopate. I saw, too, that, especially in France, the old Gallican doctrine was being more and more supplanted and was falling into disrepute, while, simultaneously, perfect unbelief was making gigantic strides there. A presentiment of what events and circumstances we might encounter took possession of me, and, for my own instruction and assurance, I conceived the necessity of devoting myself to a thorough and comprehensive study of the question, and, above all, to examine the sources themselves. At the same time, my mind was busied with the thought that I might, perhaps, be able to fill up a much-felt gap in literature, and to produce a history of the Papacy that would satisfy the scientific requirements of the present day. By working steadily for many years, I have thus brought together materials which are more extensive and complete than are to be found in any printed work. I do not think that any evidence of weight has escaped me. The result was the consciousness that I had a clear survey of this subject in its course of development through fifteen centuries, and had reached that certainty which is at all attainable in the department of history,—and, in consequence, I also won the conviction that I must renounce the plan of a history of the popes, for the book would undoubtedly have at once found its way into the Index, when I should have been obliged, according to the new practice introduced by Herr von Scherr, either to make an untrue recantation or give up my academical activity as teacher, to which I clung with all my soul.

As to the question of dogma, for me it was now clear and certain that the whole edifice of papal omnipotence and infallibility rested on cunning and deceit, on compulsion and violence in manifold forms, and that the building-stones with which this edifice has been raised were taken from a series of forgeries and fictions, with the conclusions and consequences founded on them,—a series which stretches through all the centuries since the fifth.

Here I now stand, and your Grace may yourself imagine with what feelings I must accept such suggestions as yours, and those the present pope has sent to me three times already. I say to myself daily that I am a frail man, constantly prone to err in many ways. At the bottom, the whole of my mental life has been a continual correcting and laying aside of earlier formed opinions and views. I am conscious that I have never obstinately closed my eyes to a better judgment; at all events, I cannot call such a case to mind. Though at first with a heavy heart, I have renounced even cherished ideas as soon as it was clear to me that they were untenable. Now it is, of course, possible that a derangement of my mind has set in, which makes me incapable of understanding historical facts. Instances of such a condition, even in celebrated men, do exist. With me, then, this distemper must be already very old, for since, perhaps, 1857, *i.e.* since my return from my journey to Rome, I have always cherished the same conviction in reference to the points at issue. Should this be the case with me, the public discussion I so much desired and prayed for would have been the best remedy, if not for me, at all events for those numerous individuals who, in the matter in question, have set their confidence in my knowledge and love of truth, and who would certainly have been undeceived by the disclosure of my condition, and led back again to the great community.

You, Most Reverend Sir, it is true, seem to cherish a still worse view of my mental condition. You exhort me to think of my soul's salvation, and I meet this earnest admonition with reverential thankfulness. In a mild and gentle form you mean to say to me, "If you die without recanting, you will of a certainty go to hell, to everlasting damnation, for, at all events since 1871, you have been living persistently in deadly sin; your condition is not an involuntary straying or a disturbed mental faculty, but obduracy and demoniacal infatuation." Should this really be my condition, it would certainly be much more appropriate to practise an exorcism on me than to make an attempt to convert me by a convincing religious conference.

But I beg you to consider that it is here a question not only of myself, but of thousands of persons, for whom the exposure of my errors and the explanation of obscure Church doctrines would have just such consequences as your Grace is so very desirous to see.

That which can be done for the attainment of your object lies in your own hand. Choose out one, or even several, of the clergy of your diocese, which is surely rich enough in learned men; I am ready to meet one and all, and the only condition I make, really a very natural one, is that two shorthand writers be admitted, in order to report the speeches *pro* and *con*, and that these reports be then printed and published. If I am refuted, I solemnly promise to submit at once and to recant. I shall then employ the remainder of my life that may be allotted to me in refuting my own writings.

You, Most Reverend Sir, are, as I understand from your letter, perfectly (*fide divina*) convinced that the newly-made Articles of Faith, now seventeen years old, contain self-evident truth, and, accordingly, the exposure of the nullity of the numerous objections brought forward against them is a matter of no great difficulty. He whom you choose will, of course, think so too, and will therefore advance to meet an old and feeble man of eighty-eight with the calm certainty of victory. For it is not a question of the mysteries of faith, as the Trinity and the Incarnation, about which we can dispute until doomsday, and that to no purpose. We here stand on the firm foundation of history, of evidences and of facts. These are things which can be cleared up and expounded in such a way that every well-educated and well-instructed man can form his own judgment of the justice or injustice of the one side or the other, even without having gone through any course of theology.

I know perfectly well that my offer will meet with

the greatest opposition on the part of your Ordinariate, for, as is well known, the latter is wont to act according to the principle of refusing every one who begs an audience, and of at once hurling at him the bolt of excommunication. But I pray you to reflect that this method of procedure is contrary to the truly ecclesiastical one. You are yourself well aware that episcopal Synods were frequently summoned in order to give one who was accused of heresy an opportunity of explaining and defending his views. Of this there are plenty of instances. With Pelagius, a simple layman, negotiations were carried on at several Synods for six years, evident as his heresy was, until at length his exclusion from the community of the Church ensued. How many other names, too, might be mentioned here, even out of much later times! You are well aware when and how this fair and just manner of procedure was altered. It was still observed in the case of Abelard and others in the twelfth century, but in the thirteenth the popes established the Inquisition, with secret procedure, prescribed torture, *carcer durus*, and excruciating forms of execution, as means of conversion, and gave orders that torture should be resorted to on simple suspicion. At Constance, however, Huss and Jerome were still permitted to plead their cause fully and in detail; then, and not until then, was it that they were burned at the stake. The Ordinariate has, I must admit, the papal theory and practice on its side, and will undoubtedly say, that, now, under the rule of force and papal infallibility, its manner of proceeding is perfectly correct. Nevertheless, methinks, it would have been becoming to treat the old man, who for nearly half a century had served the Church faithfully, rather in the spirit of the older Church than in that of the age of the Inquisition and decretals, and, at the very least, to give him a hearing. You, Most Reverend Sir, tell me that my submission will be a cause of rejoicing for millions of believers. If millions really take any interest in my person and my fate, they would surely also have taken it in good part had my case been disposed of in a less tyrannical and precipitate manner. I know only one other diocese where I should probably have been treated as in Munich, namely, in Ratisbon; but what a different course things would have taken had I passed through the crisis in Vienna, Prague, Bamberg, or Rottenburg!

Friends and those who are conversant with history have often told me I should reflect that no ecclesiastical system was more despised on account of the frightful abuse to which it was put than excommunication. For had it not been calculated that formerly —for instance in the fourteenth century—half the number of all Christians were excommunicated; that thousands remained under the ban for years on account of a debt of a few shillings; further, that it was not a rare occurrence for whole nations to be laid under an interdict on account of a single man; that the Church had allowed to be forced upon her the papal doctrine that millions of believers could and might be deprived for years of the gifts bestowed upon them by Christ, if a prince, for example, had done anything to displease the Papal See! I said to myself that to be excommunicated was quite an ordinary circumstance, for the most part unregarded by those affected, so that the Roman Curia in its formularies containing promotions or other favours, had inserted a clause which has special reference to the fact of excommunication. At the same time I knew, of course, that according to the teaching of the Fathers, an unjust ban redounds to the one concerned as a blessing and not as a curse. Yet I will not deny that such an obvious endeavour to abandon me to the hatred of the people and the attacks of fanatics affected me painfully, for was it not in consequence of the measures decreed by the Ordinariate that the Chief of the Police warned me formally to be on my guard, as they had knowledge of an act of violence that was to be perpetrated on me!

Thank God, these things are now long past! At that time a feeling of shame came over me to think that such a spectacle of *odium theologicum*, raised to a pitch of paroxysm, should be displayed in the eyes of the German nation and of the adherents of other confessions. From that moment I was silent in spite of the severest temptation to speak. But your Grace will easily understand that the mere thought of entering again into any relation with the authors of these things has now something repulsive and painful about it for me. The effect produced by this method of procedure was, however, the opposite of the one intended. They wanted to arouse enemies on every hand, and goad on the hatred of the people against me. The clerical daily press, which is so well known to you, received *carte blanche* against me. Yet this was all in vain. In a short time the number of those who, at home and abroad, gave me signs of their good-will and sympathy was more than trebled; but what had still greater value for me, was the fact that not a single one of my friends forsook me. Not one of the men whose good opinion I valued has turned away from me. Nay rather, the number of these well-wishers and friends is constantly increasing, even in ecclesiastical circles; and your Grace, I suppose, would be very much surprised if I were to inform you how many of our equals give me their assent, or let it be guessed. How could it be otherwise? The new dogmas have been introduced by force and violence, and it is by force and violence that they must be constantly maintained.

One more point I must refer to as a supplement to the confession I have herewith made to you. It concerns the oath, which like all priests I had to take, by order of the Church, to expound the Holy Scriptures only according to the consensus of the Fathers and according to the sense imputed to them by the ancient Church—"item sacram scripturam juxta cum sensum, quem tenuit ac tenet sancta mater ecclesia . . . admitto nec eam unquam nisi juxta unanimem consensum patrum accipiam et interpretabor,"[1] says the text. It seems to me that those who acknowledge the Vatican Articles of Faith are thereby guilty of downright perjury. For it is notorious that the exposition given at Rome in 1870 to the passages which were quoted as biblical proof, differs entirely from that of the Fathers, and has not been advanced by a single one of the commentators that belong to the early patristic age. I have asked several of our equals how they are able to make such an act of perjury harmonise with their consciences. The answer was always an evasive one, or an embarrassed shrug of the shoulder. They said that this was a question of detail which the individual priest or layman did not need to enter into. Or they said that the very essence and merit of believing consisted precisely in giving one's self up blindly and implicitly to the

[1] "In the same way I acknowledge the Holy Scriptures according to the sense which the Holy Mother Church has maintained and still maintains . . . and I shall never understand and expound them in any other way than according to the unanimous agreement of the Fathers."

powers that be, and in leaving it to them to settle any contradiction that might exist. I do not need to tell you what an impression deplorable subterfuges of this kind have made upon me, and accordingly, at the very beginning of the way you bid me take, there lies a stone which I am unable either to remove or surmount. For I should have to swear this form of oath over again, with the additions of the Vatican Council inserted by the Papal See, and thus, so to say, in one breath call upon God to witness that I was willing to believe and teach a dogma and its contrary at the same time. Can you seriously exact anything of this sort from me? Am I to appear before the eternal Judge with a double perjury on my conscience?

I cannot help conjecturing that your Grace has addressed your letter to me at the instigation of colleagues, or because you were moved to it by influence from abroad. Should this be the case, you will perhaps be desirous that a public testimony of your having fulfilled your duty should be presented to the world. If so, I am quite ready to give publicity to this my answer, and would (of course only with your express permission) have your letter prefixed to it. I am all the more ready to do so, as for some time past I have had the feeling that in this highly important matter, which more or less affects the whole of mankind, I have kept silence too long, and have left the public in uncertainty about the present state of my convictions.

Your Grace has, of course, no time, nor would you find it becoming your high dignity, to give your special attention to instructing and convincing me. But should any one out of the numerous circle of learned theologians who are at your disposal undertake this charge, I promise beforehand to have his reply printed with mine, but, of course, with the addition of any responses of my own.

A great deal more might still be said and expressly emphasised in the interest of the Church—that is, if she is seriously to be or become a *columna veritatis;* I should then add something on this subject to my defence.—I remain, yours most respectfully and obediently,

J. VON DÖLLINGER.

P.S.—I have just noticed that it might appear as though the last proposal does not harmonise with the one previously made, or is to replace it. It still is and remains my earnest desire and request, which I address to your Grace with all deference, that I may be allowed an oral defence and explanation of my position. In this case my letter shall be at the same time my text, convenient and suitable to be used by my opponent and myself as a foundation for the discussion.

XXIV.

ARCHBISHOP VON STEICHELE TO DÖLLINGER.

(March 19th, 1887.)

REVEREND PROVOST AND REICHSRATH,—In your letter to me of the 1st inst., among other things you say: "I cannot help conjecturing that your Grace has addressed your letter to me at the instigation of colleagues, or because you were moved to it by influence from abroad." This passage of your letter requires a correction. Rest assured that I did not take that step at the instigation of colleagues, or because I was moved to it by influence from abroad. The thought of once more addressing myself to you sprang from my own heart; I carried it out with the feeling of my duty, and out of love to you. You must kindly excuse my entering into details on any other points of your letter. Always bearing the same love to you.—I remain, yours truly,

ANTONIUS,
Archbishop of Munich and Freising.

XXV.

NUNCIO RUFFO SCILLA TO DÖLLINGER.

(October 1st, 1887.[1])

Munich le 1 Octobre 1887.

Très-illustre Docteur! Ceci est un billet tout-à-fait privé et reservé dont personne a été mis à part. Je veux me donner le plaisir de vous l'écrire puisque je pense que peut-être il vous sera agréable d'apprendre mes sentiments à l'égard de votre personne.

Si la très-sáinte Vièrge du Rosaire et votre bon ange gardien vous inspirent de donner à l'Église une très-grande consolation en la circostance de la grande fête de famille que nous allons avoir pour le jubilé de notre saint Père, je suis là tout-à-fait à votre disposition.

Comme Sa Saintété a bien voulu me confier sa représentance en Bavière, je desire très-vivement que la plus grande joie Lui parvienne du Royaume de Marie et qu'un' autre grand fête se solennise parmi les innombrables savants et amis qui vous aiment comme celui à qui ils doivent leur science.

[1] Printed exactly as in the manuscript.

Je vous prie, très-illustre M. le Docteur, d'agréer l'assurence de mes meilleurs sentiments.

✠ L. Archevêque de Petra,
Nonce apostolique.

TRANSLATION.

Most illustrious Doctor,—This note is an altogether private and confidential one, of which no one has any knowledge. I wish to give myself the pleasure of writing it to you, as I think you will perhaps be pleased to learn my feelings in regard to you personally.

If, on the occasion of the great family festival which we are going to celebrate at the jubilee of our Holy Father, the Most Blessed Virgin of the Rosary, and your good guardian angel, prompt you to offer the Church a very great consolation, I am quite at your disposal.

As His Holiness has been pleased to repose confidence in me as his representative in Bavaria, I am very desirous that his greatest joy may come from the Kingdom of Mary, and that another great festival may be celebrated by the innumerable scholars and friends who love you as him to whom they are indebted for the knowledge they possess.

I beg you, illustrious Doctor, be assured of my kindly feeling.

✠ L. Archbishop of Petra,
Apostolic Nuncio.

XXVI.

DÖLLINGER TO NUNCIO RUFFO SCILLA.

(October 12th, 1887.)

Monseigneur! A mon âge ce sont surtout les idées d'une mort prochaine et de ce qui doit suivre cette catastrophe, qui se présentent à l'esprit. Mon principal soin est, comme cela doit être, de mettre ma conscience en repos et sûreté. Frappé d'excommunication par un prélat, qui pour cet acte a été comblé d'éloges par Pie IX., j'ai senti depuis seize ans le besoin impérieux de me négliger rien de ce qui pourrait contribuer à m'éclaircir sur la conduite à tenir dans une situation si pénible. J'aurais pu commettre des forfaits nombreux qu'on ne m'en aurait pas puni, car la discipline cléricale en Allemagne est extrêmement indulgente; mais le crime qu'on m'imputait, était d'une énormité inouie : je refusais de changer ma foi, je refusais de croire et de professer un nouveau dogme, dont le contraire m'avait été enseigné dans ma jeunesse et dont je connaissais la fausseté par 56 ans d'études et de recherches. Cela suffisait pour infliger à un vieillard de 72 ans, qui jusque-là n'avait encouru ni reproche ni blâme, une peine qui selon la doctrine de l'église est pire que la mort.

Permettez-moi ici, Monseigneur, de citer quelques faits personnels ; peut-être qu'ils serviront à mitiger tant soi peu la sévérité de votre jugement.

J'ai été professeur actif de théologie pendant 47 ans, de 1823 jusqu'à 1871. Pendant cette longue période j'ai toujours enseigné le contraire de ce qui a été décidé par Pie IX. en 1870 ; tout le monde savait ou pouvait savoir ce que je croyais et professais sur cette question ; les différents nonces apostoliques qui se sont succédés ici, ne pouvaient guère l'ignorer ; ils me traitaient tous avec bienveillance, et ni eux ni aucun évêque allemand ou français ou anglais ne m'ont jamais dit un mot ou m'ont donné un avertissement quelconque, qui m'aurait fait connaître qu'ils étaient mécontents de mon enseignement. J'enseignais ce que j'avais appris de mes maîtres, ce qui m'avait été confirmé par mes recherches, et ce que j'avais trouvé dans les ouvrages historiques et théologiques que je jugeais les plus solides : c'était que l'infaillibilité du Pape était une opinion inventée bien tard, mais actuellement tolérée dans l'église, mais que de l'imputer à tout le monde catholique, c'était, comme s'exprimait un catéchisme anglais tres-répandu, une calomnie protestante.

Je sais par quantité de témoins irréprochables,

par des aveux échappés, que le concile du Vatican n'était pas libre, qu'on y a employé les menaces, les intimidations, les séductions. Je le sais par des évêques dont je garde les lettres, ou qui me l'ont avoué de vive voix. Le même archevêque de Munich, qui ensuite m'a excommunié, est venu chez moi le lendemain de son retour de Rome et m'a raconté des détails qui ne m'ont laissé aucun doute. Il est vrai que tous ces prélats ont faits leur soumission : tous s'accordaient à dire pour excuse : " Nous ne voulons pas faire un schisme." Moi aussi, je ne veux pas être membre d'une société schismatique ; je suis isolé. Persuadé que la sentence lancée contre moi est injuste et nulle de droit, je persiste à me regarder comme membre de la grande église catholique, et c'est l'église elle-même qui, par la bouche des saints pères, me dit, qu'une telle excommunication ne peut pas nuire à mon âme.

Seize ans se sont passés depuis l'anathème dont on m'a frappé. J'ai employé ce temps à me livrer à des études et recherches réitérées, à puiser dans les sources, à suivre la tradition d'un siècle à l'autre. Un examen approfondi des témoignages prétendus, qui ont été amassés dans les ouvrages écrits en faveur du concile, m'a fait voir qu'il y a là un amas d'altérations, de fictions, de falsifications dont la plupart avaient été déjà reconnues comme telles au 17 siècle.

Maintenant, Monseigneur, que me demandez-vous? Devrais-je dire au monde: catholiques et protestants, voyez désormais en moi un homme d'une ignorance grossière qui pendant un demi-siècle s'est trompé lui-même et a trompé les autres, qui n'a reconnu la vérité qu'au bout de sa longue carrière? Les hommes qui sont capables de juger de telles questions, m'en croiraient-ils. Je sais bien ce qu'on dirait; les uns diraient: c'est un vieillard retombé en enfance (rimbambito); les autres diraient: c'est un menteur et un vil hypocrite; il doit l'avoir été pendant toute sa vie, ou il l'est à présent. Et puis mon premier devoir serait alors de refuter moi-même, mes ouvrages, ouvrages traduits en plusieurs langues, et de montrer qu'ils ne sont qu'un tissu de faussetés. Ce serait vraiment un fait unique et vous ne sauriez citer dans toute l'histoire de l'église un tour d'esprit égal à celui-là.

Et ici, Monseigneur, je me permets de vous citer un fait caractéristique. Lorsque l'archevêque, obéissant, à ce qu'il disait, aux ordres de Pape, me communiqua la sentence portée contre moi, il me fit annoncer, que j'étais assujetti à toutes les peines accumulées par le droit canonique contre les excommuniés. La première et la plus importante de ces peines est contenue dans la célèbre bulle du Pape Urbain II., qui décide qu'il est permis à tout le monde de tuer un excommunié, quand on le fait par un motif de zèle pour l'église. En même temps il fit prêcher contre moi dans toutes les chaires de Munich, et l'effet que ces déclamations produisaient, fut tel que le chef de la police me fit avertir que des attentats se tramaient contre ma personne, et que je ferais bien de ne pas sortir sans accompagnement. Oserais-je soulever la question, Monseigneur, si, en cas de ma soumission, je serais obligé de déclarer au monde que je trouve cette décision du Pape infaillible parfaitement conforme à la morale évangélique ?

Je ne vous ai fait entrevoir qu'une partie des raisons qui me forcent à renoncer à l'idée d'une révocation ou soumission ; j'en ai encore beaucoup d'autres. Mais ce que j'ai écrit ici, suffira, me semble-t-il, pour vous faire comprendre, qu'avec de telles convictions on peut être dans un état de paix intérieure et de tranquillité d'esprit, même au seuil de l'éternité.

Agréez, Monseigneur, l'expression du profond respect, avec lequel je signe

J. DÖLLINGER.

TRANSLATION.

Most Reverend Sir, — At my age it is the thought of an approaching death, and of what must follow this catastrophe, that especially press themselves on the mind. My principal care is, as it ought to be, to set my conscience at rest and in safety. Laid under sentence of excommunication by a prelate who for this act was overwhelmed with eulogies by Pius IX., I have felt now for sixteen years the imperious necessity of neglecting nothing that could contribute towards throwing light on the line of conduct to be observed in such a painful situation. I might have committed numerous transgressions without having been punished for them, because clerical discipline in Germany is extremely indulgent; but the crime imputed to me was of an unheard-of enormity. I refused to change my faith; I refused to believe and teach a new dogma, the contrary of which I had been taught in my youth, and the falsity of which I had learned by the study and research of fifty-six years. This was sufficient to inflict on an old man of seventy-two, who up to that time had incurred neither reproach nor blame, a punishment which, according to the teaching of the Church, is worse than death.

Permit me, Most Reverend Sir, to cite here a few personal facts. Perhaps they will serve somewhat to mitigate the severity of your judgment.

For forty-seven years, from 1823 to 1871, I was an active professor of theology. During this long period I always taught the contrary of what was decided by Pius IX. in 1870. The whole world knew or might have known what I believed and taught on this question. The various apostolic nuncios who succeeded one another here could scarcely be in ignorance of it. They all treated me with benevolence, and neither they nor any German, French, or English bishop ever said a word to me, or gave me any intimation, from which I could have gathered that they were dissatisfied with my teaching. I taught what I had learned from my masters, what had been confirmed by my researches, and what I had found in the historical and theological works which I judged to be the most reliable, namely, that the infallibility of the pope was an opinion that had appeared at a very late period, but which was now tolerated in the Church; but that to ascribe it to the whole Catholic world would be, as a widely circulated English catechism expressed it, "a Protestant calumny."

From many irreproachable witnesses, and from confessions which escaped them, I know that the Vatican Council was not free, and that they employed menaces, intimidations, and seductions there. I know it from bishops whose letters I have, or who have confessed it to me orally.

The same Archbishop of Munich who afterwards excommunicated me, came to my house on the day after his return from Rome, and related details to me which left no doubt on the point. It is true all these prelates have made their submission; they all excused their conduct by saying: "We do not wish to cause a schism." Nor do I wish to be a member of a schismatic society: I am isolated. Convinced that the sentence decreed against me is unjust and legally null, I persist in regarding myself as a member of the great Catholic Church; and it is the Church herself, who, through her holy Fathers, tells me that such an excommunication cannot harm my soul.

Sixteen years have passed since the anathema was pronounced against me. This time I have employed in devoting myself to renewed study and research, in drawing from the sources, and in following tradition from one century to another. A thorough examination of the alleged testimonies, which have been gathered in the works written in favour of the Council, has shown me that it is here a question of a mass of alterations, fictions, and forgeries, the greater part of which had been already recognised as such in the seventeenth century.

And now, Most Reverend Sir, what do you require of me? Am I to say to the world: "Catholics and Protestants, behold in me henceforth a man of gross ignorance, who for half a century has been deceiving himself and others, and who has only recognised the truth at the end of his long career?" Would those who are capable of judging in such questions believe me? I know well what they would say. Some would say, "He has fallen into his dotage." Others, "He is a liar and a vile hypocrite: he must have been one during his whole life, or he is one now." And then my first duty would be to refute myself and my works,—works which are translated into several languages,—and to show that they are only a tissue of errors. This would indeed be a unique fact, and you would not be able to cite from the whole history of the Church any mental change like it.

And here, Most Reverend Sir, I take the liberty of citing a characteristic fact. When the Archbishop, according to his own words, obeying the orders of the pope, communicated to me the sentence that had been pronounced against me, he informed me that I had incurred all the punishments which are heaped by the canonical law upon those who are excommunicated. The first and most important of these punishments is contained in the celebrated Bull of Pope Urban II., which decides that every one may put to death one who is excommunicated, when it is done from a motive of zeal for the Church. At the same time he had sermons preached against me from all the pulpits of Munich, and the effect produced by these declamations was such that the Chief of the Police informed me that attacks were being plotted against me, and that I should do well not to go out without company. May I dare, Most Reverend Sir, to raise the question whether, in case I should submit, I should be obliged to declare to the world that I consider this decision of the infallible pope in perfect harmony with the morals of the gospel?

I have only intimated a few of the reasons which compel me to renounce the idea of a recantation or submission. I have still many others; but what I have written here will, I think, suffice in order to make intelligible to you that with such convictions one can be in a state of inward peace and tranquillity of mind even on the threshold of eternity.

Accept, Most Reverend Sir, the expression of profound respect with which I sign myself

J. DÖLLINGER.

XXVII.

NUNCIO RUFFO SCILLA TO DÖLLINGER.

(October 14th, 1887.[1])

TRÈS-ILLUSTRE PROFESSEUR ! Je vous en prie, ne m'accusez pas de sévérité ! Que Dieu me garde de traiter ainsi mon prochain !

Je suis isolé, vous dites.—Voilà le mot désolant, la triste position de laquelle nous desirons touts de vous voir sorti.—Mais ce n'est certellement pas moi qui pourrà vous décider à la courageuse resolution ; c'est au contraire Notre Seigneur, qui est le *Roi de coeurs.* Vous ajoutez que la serait un frait vraiment unique dans l'histoire, vues les circostances du passé. — Tant mieux, cher Professeur : vous êtes donc à même de procurer à l'Église une joie unique et à votre âme un mérite énorme. Quant'aux quelques imbecilles (permettez-moi ce mot), qui oseraient vous juger comme vous le craignez, ils seraient mis bien vite à leur place, soyez en sur. Eux seulement pourraient affirmer que vous avez pendant des années *trompé le monde.* Puisque, avant 1870, vous

---

[1] Printed exactly as in the manuscript.

aviez avec vous touts les antifaillibilites qui dans l'enceinte et dehors du Concil userent de leur droit d'opposition avec liberté et même avec violence. Tandisque votre si penible insolement après juillet 1870 vous prouve que tout le monde catholique est convencu que vous êtes dans l'erreur. Faites-vous donc moins cas du monde catholique que des imbecilles?

Que rien donc vous trouble, très-illustre Professeur, si vous voulez sortir de votre isolement. Confiez-vous d'abord très-ouvertement à N. S. Père le Pape. Vous savez bien que d'autres celebrités ont eu à s'applaudir de leur confiance en ce grand Pontife. Vous serez fier de votre soummission et la grande famille catholique en celebrant le Jubilé du Père verra a ses coté le Fils bien aimé.

En attendant je suis toujours disposé à vous rendre service et vous être util en vous priant de croir à mon affection toute particulière.

✠ L. Archevêque de Petra,
Nonce apostolique.
Ce 14. Octobre 1887.

TRANSLATION.

Most Illustrious Professor,—I beg you not to accuse me of severity! God forbid I should treat my neighbour so!

"I am isolated," you say. Those are comfortless words, and it is the sad position from which we all wish to see you escape. But it is certainly not I who can move you to the courageous resolve. Our Lord, who is the *King of hearts*, alone can do it. You add that this would be a really unique fact in history with respect to the circumstances of the past. All the better, dear Professor. You are thus in a position to procure for the Church a unique joy, and for your soul an extraordinary degree of merit. As for the few imbeciles (permit me the use of this word) who would dare to judge you, as you fear, be sure of this, that they would very soon be shown their place. They alone could assert that you had been deceiving the world for years. For before 1870 you had on your side all anti-infallibilists who, within and without the Council, made use of their right of opposition with freedom, and even with violence, while your very painful isolation since July 1870 proves to you that the whole Catholic world is convinced you are in error. Do you then esteem the Catholic world more lightly than imbeciles?

Let nothing trouble you then, Most Illustrious Professor, if you are willing to forsake your isolation. First of all, unbosom yourself freely to our Holy Father the pope. You are well aware that other celebrities have had reason to congratulate themselves on their confidence in this great High Priest. You will be proud of your submission, and the great Catholic family at the celebration of the Jubilee of the Father will see the well-beloved son at his side.

In the meantime I am always ready to render you any service and be of any use to you, and I beg you to believe in my special affection for you.

✠ L. Archbishop of Petra,
Apostolic Nuntio.
October 14*th*, 1887.

APPENDIX.

DÖLLINGER TO A DIGNITARY OF THE CHURCH.

(February 7th, 1868.[1])

REVEREND SIR,—Your letter lays me under the obligation of expressing my warmest thanks to you, for—in spite of all that has been said and done—it still betrays such a friendly disposition that it would be a sin to place the slightest doubt in its pure and sincere intention.

Hence, how gladly would I fulfil your request, and follow your counsel, if I could only do so without wounding my convictions!

You require that I should make a public protest against the abuse to which Herr Scholl has subjected my name. He has named me in the same breath with Galileo, Fénelon, Hirscher, etc. etc., in

---

[1] The letter to which this is an answer has unfortunately not been found among Döllinger's literary remains.

[It has since been found, and was written by Dr. Westermayer, Rector of St. Peter's, Munich.—TRANSLATOR.]

short with those who have been ill-treated or censured by the Roman Curia. Now I have experienced neither the one nor the other. Hitherto, my writings have not yet been placed on the Index. Accordingly I do not belong to the above-named society. It is true I could have this printed in a couple of words. But such a declaration would probably not satisfy you yourself, much less others. The contributors and readers, for instance, of the *Volksbote*, of the *Donauzeitung*, and other "well-affected" papers would say: "If Döllinger is not yet condemned, it is only an oversight on the part of Rome, for he has merited it long ago." You know our "Ultramontanes of the purest water," as they now title themselves in the *Pastoralblatt*, and what they think of my writings and their author. But people in general would say: "Why trouble the public with a declaration about something every one already knows, *i.e.* every one who has any interest in these matters?" Besides this, for many years I have experienced a steadily growing dislike to sending any notice concerning my person to the daily papers. I have done it but seldom, and every time I have rued it afterwards. I know of a certainty that if I were now to meet your wishes, I should repent of it within a few days.

You require that I should come out of the sulky corner into which I have withdrawn. In this way you describe me as a man who simply exists, and in gloomy inactivity broods over insults, real and supposed. This is by no means the condition of my mind. I do what I have always done. I follow the course of affairs calmly and attentively, and I strive daily to supplement and correct my knowledge. It is quite true that much of what is now done in the name of the Catholic religion fills me with pain and sometimes with indignation, and that it frequently seems to me as though the Church were being worse treated by her supposed friends and protectors than by her declared adversaries. But do you call this "sulking"? If so, then St. Bernard, Fénelon—and how many others!—were also in sulky corners in their time.

Further, according to your views and requirements, I am to give a public assurance of my submissiveness to the Papal See. Well, I think you know the proverb, and have often proved the truth of it—"Qui s'excuse, s'accuse." " Habemus confitentem reum, ex ore tuo te judico, serve nequam," would be the general cry of that party which has for its exponents and teachers the *Volksbote* and the *Donauzeitung*, "the Ultramontanes of the purest water," as they now call themselves in well-merited self-confidence. Do you believe, then, that these people would ever forgive me for having been so audacious as to have had my own convictions now and then, which were not quite identical with the present current opinion in Rome, and to have given utterance to them? Never! I know with whom I have to deal.[1] In these circles they say of me irrevocably: "Hic niger est, hunc tu, *Romane,* caveto!" You yourself would be astounded, I think, if you knew by whom and for what reasons I have been denounced in Rome. I could tell you some pretty stories about it! I suppose you yourself know something about the fate of the Assembly of Catholic scholars, which must now, of course, remain a unicum. What we undertook at that time was done with fullest consent and even sympathy of three bishops, and among them our own archbishop. We all believed, forsooth, that we had acted in the best interests of the Church; and how did Rome reward us, especially me, for it? To think of all I had to hear about my boldness and arrogance in inviting German scholars to a conference! And all this burst over me, *notâ bene,* in consequence of *German* denunciation and incitements!

What, I should like to know, would my old friends and fellow-combatants, Moehler and Goerres, have said had they lived to see such things? I know what they would have said. I know that both of them—the one more sharply, the other more mildly—would have said to those who to-day call themselves the true Ultramontanes: "Away with you!

---

[1] [Lit.: "I know my Pappenheimers." An allusion to Schiller's *Wallensteins Tod,* iii. 15.—TRANSLATOR.]

Quid nobis et vobis? You are a race with which we have no dealings."

After having devoted oneself, as I have done, for over fifty years to the study of history, and after becoming thoroughly absorbed in the past, one must at last surely have learned something of an historical Nemesis, and of the connection between cause and effect. I have studied the history of Spain, and hence the events that have just taken place there did not surprise me. On this subject I could easily write an instructive book which would clear up many things, but shall not do so. Well, of late years Rome has had much urgent business with Spain, and of what nature was it? First: The pope, as a token of his special favour, and in recognition of her services, sent the Golden Rose to ... (Queen Isabella).... Second: Only very recently, at an open meeting of the Consistory, he delivered a eulogy on the Inquisition, and declared it to be an excellent, beneficial, and genuinely ecclesiastical institution. You will have read this in the *Pastoralblatt*. Third: He has canonized an inquisitor, and recommended all Spaniards to honour this man in future as a pattern of Christian virtues, and as worthy of imitation. Spain has just given her answer to this threefold allocution, and will give it again. Yes, there is a Nemesis!

What is your opinion, Honoured Sir and Patron? If I were now, after all, to give a public assurance of my devotedness and submission to the Roman See, which would, of course, be without conditions and without limitations, should I not, in order to leave no room for any more doubt, have to give expression also to my most submissive adhesion to the eulogy on the Inquisition, and to the canonisation of Don Pedro de Arbues? Should I not have to say: "Hitherto, it is true, in agreement with all who have made a study of Spanish history, I was of opinion that the Inquisition had brought an unspeakably large amount of harm to Spain; but since the publication of that allocution I at once gave up my opinion, and from this time forward I shall maintain against any and every man, 'Roma locuta est,' the Inquisition is excellent, and Spain could not do better than re-introduce it?" You know that whoever says A must also say B. I am curious to know your opinion and your advice.

In conclusion, a word about Dr. Pichler. It is sufficient to remark that I have seen him but once within three months, and then only for five minutes, on the occasion of his announcing to me the visit of a foreign gentleman, who wished to be introduced by him. This is the sum-total of my contact with that man.

From this letter, which has become somewhat long, you will at least be able to conclude that I lay great value on maintaining your friendly and favourable disposition towards me. I have given you deeper glimpses into my inner life, into my thoughts and motives, than I am wont to allow others. Refute me where you see I am in error. You know I do not close my mind to the censure and correction of my opinions.

Finally, I must beg you to please return me this letter at your convenience after you have read it. I have no copy of it, and I might easily happen to be so situated that I should be obliged to give an explanation of my present position to others.

Totus tuus,
J. DÖLLINGER.

P.S.—As a token of my sincere and friendly affection, I send you along with this letter the second edition of a book[1] with which you are already acquainted. A few additions have been made here and there.

[1] Undoubtedly *The First Age of Christianity and the Church*.

T. and T. Clark's Publications.

HISTORY OF THE CHRISTIAN CHURCH.

By PHILIP SCHAFF, D.D., LL.D.

New Edition, Re-written and Enlarged.

1. **APOSTOLIC CHRISTIANITY, A.D. 1–100.** Two Vols. Ex. demy 8vo. price 21s.
2. **ANTE-NICENE CHRISTIANITY, A.D. 100–325.** Two Vols. Ex. demy 8vo, price 21s.
3. **NICENE AND POST-NICENE CHRISTIANITY, A.D. 325–600.** Two Vols. Ex. demy 8vo, price 21s.
4. **MEDIÆVAL CHRISTIANITY, A.D. 590–1073.** Two Vols. Ex. demy 8vo. price 21s. (Completion of this Period, 1073–1517, in preparation.)
5. **MODERN CHRISTIANITY** The German Reformation, A.D. 1517–1530. Two Vols. Ex. demy 8vo, price 21s.

'*Dr. Schaff's "History of the Christian Church" is the most valuable contribution to Ecclesiastical History that has ever been published in this country. When completed it will have no rival in point of comprehensiveness, and in presenting the results of the most advanced scholarship and the latest discoveries. Each division covers a separate and distinct epoch, and is complete in itself.*'

'We have read these volumes with the most unmingled satisfaction. . . . For the student, who wants to get at facts, to understand the *rationale* of the facts, and to have the means of verifying them, there is no book so good as this.'—*Church Bells.*

In Three Volumes, demy 8vo, price 12s. each,

A HISTORY OF THE COUNCILS OF THE CHURCH.

FROM THE ORIGINAL DOCUMENTS.

TRANSLATED FROM THE GERMAN OF
C. J. HEFELE, D.D., BISHOP OF ROTTENBURG.

VOL. I. TO A.D. 325.
VOL. II. A.D. 326 TO 429.
VOL. III. A.D. 429 TO THE CLOSE OF THE COUNCIL OF CHALCEDON.

'This careful translation of Hefele's Councils.'—Dr. PUSEY.

'A thorough and fair compendium, put in a most accessible and intelligent form.'—*Guardian.*

'A work of profound erudition, and written in a most candid spirit. The book will be a standard work on the subject.'—*Spectator.*

'The most learned historian of the Councils.'—*Père Gratry.*

'We cordially commend Hefele's Councils to the English student.'—*John Bull.*

T. and T. Clark's Publications.

In Twenty-four handsome 8vo Volumes, Subscription price £6, 6s.,

ANTE-NICENE CHRISTIAN LIBRARY.

A COLLECTION OF ALL THE WORKS OF THE FATHERS OF THE CHRISTIAN CHURCH PRIOR TO THE COUNCIL OF NICÆA.

EDITED BY PROFESSOR ALEXANDER ROBERTS, D.D., AND
PROFESSOR J. DONALDSON, LL.D.

CONTENTS:—Apostolic Fathers, one vol.; Justin Martyr, Athenagoras, one vol.; Tatian, Theophilus, The Clementine Recognitions, one vol.; Clement of Alexandria, two vols.; Irenæus and Hippolytus, three vols.; Tertullian against Marcion; Cyprian, two vols.; Origen, two vols.; Tertullian, three vols.; Methodius, etc., one vol.; Apocryphal Gospels, Acts, and Revelations, one vol.; Clementine Homilies, Apostolical Constitutions, one vol.; Arnobius, one vol.; Dionysius, Gregory Thaumaturgus, Syrian Fragments, one vol.; Lactantius, two vols.; Early Liturgies and Remaining Fragments, one vol.

Any Volume may be had separately, price 10s. 6d.,—with the exception of ORIGEN,
Vol. II., 12s.; *and the* EARLY LITURGIES, 9s.

In Fifteen Volumes, demy 8vo, Subscription price £3, 19s.,

THE WORKS OF ST. AUGUSTINE.

EDITED BY MARCUS DODS, D.D.

CONTENTS:—The 'City of God,' two vols.; Writings in connection with the Donatist Controversy, one vol.; The Anti-Pelagian Writings, three vols.; 'Letters,' two vols.; Treatises against Faustus the Manichæan, one vol.; The Harmony of the Evangelists, and the Sermon on the Mount, one vol.; On the Trinity, one vol.; Commentary on John, two vols.; On Christian Doctrine, Enchiridion, On Catechising, and On Faith and the Creed, one vol.; 'Confessions,' with Copious Notes by Rev. J. G. PILKINGTON.

Any Work may be had separately, price 10s. 6d. per Volume.

SELECTION FROM
ANTE-NICENE LIBRARY AND ST. AUGUSTINE'S WORKS.

THE Ante-Nicene Library being now completed in 24 Volumes, and the St. Augustine Series being also complete (*with the exception of the* 'LIFE') in 15 Volumes, Messrs. CLARK will, as in the case of the Foreign Theological Library, give a Selection of 12 Volumes from both of those series at the *Subscription price* of THREE GUINEAS (or a larger number at same proportion).

www.ingramcontent.com/pod-product-compliance
Lightning Source LLC
Chambersburg PA
CBHW020242170426
43202CB00008B/197